Contents

PART 2   ARTICULATING THE VALUES OF YOUR ORGANIZATION   83

50
HIGH-IMPACT
Speeches
and
Remarks

THE INDISPENSABLE HANDBOOK FOR BUSINESS LEADERS

PROVEN WORDS YOU CAN ADAPT FOR ANY BUSINESS OCCASION

John Kador

Foreword by Lee Iacocca

McGraw-Hill

New York / Chicago / San Francisco / Lisbon / London / Madrid / Mexico City
Milan / New Delhi / San Juan / Seoul / Singapore / Sydney / Toronto

1 2 3 4 5 6 7 8 9 0   DOC/DOC   0 9 8 7 6 5 4

ISBN 0-07-142194-7

McGraw-Hill books are available at special quantity discounts to use as premiums and sales promotions, or for use in corporate training programs. For more information, please write to the Director of Special Sales, Professional Publishing, McGraw-Hill, Two Penn Plaza, New York, NY 10121-2298. Or contact your local bookstore.

 This book is printed on recycled, acid-free paper containing a minimum of 50% recycled, de-inked fiber.

Library of Congress Cataloging-in-Publication Data

Kador, John.
    50 high-impact speeches and remarks : proven words you can adapt for any business occasion / John Kador ; foreword by Lee Iacocca.
      p. cm.
    ISBN 0-07-142194-7 (pbk. : alk. paper)
    1. Speeches, addresses, etc.   I. Title: Fifty high-impact speeches and remarks. II. Title.
    PN6122.K33 2004
    815'.508–dc22

                              2004000165

Foreword

In my career I must have given more than 1,000 speeches. Most of the speeches I gave are long forgotten; although I hope they all accomplished the business objectives we set for them. Perhaps a few of my remarks, such as the three speeches of mine thought worthy of inclusion in this book, may serve as examples of a certain style of public speaking. A precious one or two, like the speech commemorating the centennial of the Statue of Liberty, will be with me the rest of my life. My days of making speeches are pretty much behind me, by the way. Now it's your turn.

50 High-Impact Speeches and Remarks will help you become an effective speaker by offering 50 speeches that have been used by business leaders in real-life situations. You can use these speeches as models for your own remarks. Study the speeches. Find in them the structure, rhythm, cadences, and wording that speak to your subject. Then make the speech your own.

Whenever someone asks me how to start a business speech, I have a simple answer: Start with the pure and simple truth. Of course, the truth is rarely pure and never simple. But as a business leader, your job is to tell the truth. Now, more than ever, business leaders must be seen to be telling the truth. The avalanche of corporate scandals—the Enrons, Tycos, and Worldcoms—has seriously eroded public trust in business executives. Never in my more than 50 years of management experience have I seen such loss of confidence in the honesty and basic integrity of *Fortune* 500 business executives. Regaining that trust is possible, but it will take a sustained commitment to integrity and truth.

Good news never tests an executive's commitment to the truth. It's when a leader must announce bad news—a downsizing, plant closing, or accounting irregularity—that his or her commitment to honesty and integrity is tested. And, unfortunately, business conditions today make the delivery of bad news a predictable chore for most executives.

The formula for delivering bad news is easy, even if the execution is usually painful. Here's the formula: Tell it first. Tell it straight. Tell it all.

Tell it first. A company is always better off being first to disclose a bad situation. Playing catch-up is risky. When you are the first to disclose the bad news, you set the context. You not only can talk about the problem, but also explain how and why it happened and what you are going to do about it.

Tell it straight. That means no spinning. If your company has made a decision that's dumb—like Chrysler did when it repaired cars damaged in testing and sold them as new—don't mince words and call the action "inappropriate." If it's dumb, say so.

Tell it all. That means don't leave anything out. If it's relevant to the situation, disclose it. If you don't, someone else certainly will and your whole message will be undermined.

Now, on to the speeches and remarks. I wish you the best of luck on your speech.

Lee Iacocca
Former Chairman and CEO, Chrysler
Los Angeles, California
December 2003

Preface

How to Write your Own Remarks Using This Book

This book organizes 50 of the most effective business speeches you can use as models for your own remarks.

Each of these high-impact speeches and remarks responds to a common business situation confronting every organization. Companies prosper. Or they don't. Factories open. Factories close. Products are successful. Products fizzle. Employees get promoted. Employees get terminated. Employees get married and have babies. Employees get sick and die. Every business cycle is accompanied by events in the human life cycle.

All of these events demand a public response from someone, and that someone may be you. Leaders become leaders by saying the right thing at these often difficult occasions. This book shows you how some of the most successful leaders of the past 25 years have handled similar challenges.

You will recognize many of the names associated with these speeches. But whether a speech was presented by a celebrity CEO, such as Jack Welch, or given by a lesser-known executive, the speech worked in the rough-and-tumble world of event management.

The Speech of a Thousand Words Starts with a Model

Learn from the masters. The hardest thing about preparing a speech is starting from a blank slate. But when you can start with a model speech that actually moved audiences in circumstances similar to your own, the task of writing a speech is much easier. Much of what you need to get started is probably right here: an opening, a pithy joke or anecdote, suggestions for content, ideas for rhythm and delivery, a closing. All you need is a start. Whatever your business speech challenge may be, this book offers models that you can use as a foundation for your own.

Take a look at the format of the book. To give you a peek into the secrets of professional speechwriters, each speech is presented in two columns. The left-hand column has the edited speech. The right-hand column, labeled "Talking Points," describes the rhetorical decisions that make each speech successful. Perhaps it's a matter of phrasing, rhythm, or the deliberate use of a device such as repetition, metaphor, alliteration, or oxymoron. The best speeches are all distinguished by subtle humor, innovative pacing, and other rhetorical devices. The mechanics of writing speeches are beyond the scope of this book, but studying these Talking Points is like taking a crash course in speechwriting.

The best speeches also make effective use of memorable quotations, statistics, jokes, anecdotes, and stories. The book points out how these devices, indicated with shading, advance the objectives of the speech and, if the text does not do it, identifies the sources of quotations.

Every speech also has a section called a "Scoping Document." Just as professional speechwriters provide the speaker with a short summary about the speech, its objective, and the audience, so has this information been provided for you.

Each speech selected for this book represents the highest standards of craftsmanship. Every speech met the business communications objectives for which they were crafted, and their authors are rightly satisfied with the outcomes. But even the proud authors of these speeches would hesitate to suggest that they are all perfect. Usually written under deadline pressure, speeches are generally abandoned, rarely finished. There's always room for improvement, and under the Talking Points column, I occasionally suggest an alternate wording.

Many inexperienced public speakers worry about speaking too long or not long enough. Timing a speech can be tricky. For that reason, each of these speeches includes a word count and an estimate of how long the edited speech is in minutes. For the time calculation, I use a range of 100 spoken words per minute.

Speeches Given and Speeches Yet to Be Delivered

This book may be useful to you even if you don't have an immediate speaking obligation you must honor. If you don't have an opportunity right now, chances are it won't be too long before you will be called upon to speak in public. This collection of speeches also provides inspiration on a number of business subjects for the general reader. In these pages are collected the accumulated wisdom of some of the most successful business leaders of the last

25 years. Their challenges are your challenges. Learn how they approached any number of business situations. While your business challenges may not precisely align with theirs, their approaches may offer you examples and alternatives you might not otherwise have considered.

This collection of business speeches and brief remarks can advance your career on a number of levels. The book gathers 50 high-impact speeches and remarks addressing a number of the most common business occasions and teaches you how to make your speeches and business remarks just as effective. For leaders who have a speaking engagement to prepare for, the models in this book can inspire your efforts. Attend to the wording, cadences, and structures of the masters. Then find your own voice.

Acknowledgments

For taking time out of their busy schedules, I am indebted to a number of business speech-writers and communicators. Many contributed excellent speeches for this book. I regret that I was able to include only a fraction of them.*

Mike Morrison, retired vice president of corporate communications for DaimlerChrysler and Lee Iacocca's speechwriter for 10 years, was patiently and endlessly helpful and so far has yet to submit an invoice.

Robert O. Skovgard, publisher of the Executive Speaker Company series of newsletters, unhesitatingly supported this book. The *Executive Speaker*, including the *Executive Speaker Newsletter, Executive Speeches Journal*, and most of all the The Speech Library—an archive of more than 6,000 business speeches—were resources absolutely indispensable to this book.

David Murray, editor of the *Speechwriter's Newsletter*, a Lawrence Ragan Communications publication, answered innumerable questions, made a number of invaluable introductions, and facilitated my participation in the very worthy Speechwriter's Conference, which Ragan Communications sponsors annually.

If anyone can be called a guru to the speechwriting community, that person would have to be Jerry Tarver, professor emeritus at the University of Richmond, and a recognized authority on the craft of writing speeches. I appreciate Jerry for courtesies large and small.

Margaret McBride, who helped me survive the graduate program at The American University School of Business many years ago, continues to support me in whatever I take on. Thank you, my dear Ms. McBride.

I am in the debt of the following speechwriters, communicators, and coaches: Peggy Abrahamson, Kare Anderson, Ken Askew, William Bartlett, Joanne Brown, Christopher Colford, Jim Comer, Fletcher Dean, Mike Field, Eugene Finerman, Steve Fox, Maureen

---

* Contact information for many of these individuals may be found in the List of Contributors and Resources section at the back of the book.

Herwood, Seth Hopkins, Craig L. Howe, Lee Iacocca, Peter Krass, Brian Jenner, Susan Croce Kelly, Marie Lerch, Charmaine McClarie, Mary Moreno, Karen O'Brien, Alan Perlman, Reneè Wall Rongen, Dana Rubin, Laurie Sachtleben, Steve Soltis, and Andrew Wilson.

I appreciate Richard Narramore, my editor at McGraw-Hill, for inviting me to collaborate on this project.

As always, thanks to my wife, Anna Beth Payne, and my children, Dan and Rachel, for their lack of complaint. Yet again I am humbled considering the mystery of why anyone would put up with an author as either a spouse or a dad.

John Kador
Geneva, Illinois
December 15, 2003

Introduction

1

Tap-Dancing in a Minefield: A Speechwriter's Guide to Humor

Eugene Finerman

"Humor is treacherous," says speechwriter Eugene Finerman. "It can charm, coax and persuade, but it can also distract, baffle or alienate the audience." Nevertheless humor is essential in almost every speech. So what's a speechwriter to do? In this skillful speech, Finerman demonstrates the craft of staging an after-dinner speech even as he skewers its conventions. Says Finerman, "I am both a speechwriter and a humorist, and I try not to confuse the two. I think that there is an effective use of humor in speeches, not merely as a gratuitous introduction to a speech." This speech was originally presented at a Chicago Speechwriters Forum and subsequently reprinted in The Toastmaster, *the magazine of Toastmasters International, in November 1999.*

A naked plumber walks into a bar . . . but what if you already know this joke? You will be convinced that I have nothing original to say. And what if you dislike the joke? You will be ready to hate everything else I have to say. Ah, but what if you do like the joke? Then, you will be disappointed because the rest of my speech is not about funny naked plumbers. You have just heard a coroner's report on how humor can kill a speech.

Humor is treacherous. It can charm, coax and persuade, but it can also distract, baffle or alienate the audience. All too often, jokes are added to a speech without the least regard to their relevance. No one would wedge a discussion of Byzantine art into a speech on health care. Yet, how many serious speeches begin with a warm-up of meaningless golf jokes?

Some speakers feel insecure, and they wish to ingratiate themselves with the audience. They hope that a few introductory jokes will win over the crowd. Of course, that depends if the humor is original and funny. Otherwise, the speaker will have more reason to be inse-cure. Humor is not a foolproof method of seduction. If it were, I would already be dead of syphilis.

Although we speechwriters are rumored to be ventriloquists, in fact, the dummy tells us what to write. If and when we are told to be funny, we must contend with three distinct chal-lenges: the speaker, the audience and the topic. Our jokes must reflect the speaker's per-sonality, background and affectations. I have written for a variety of characters and caricatures. One of my clients was born a chairman; his nickname at Yale was Adonis. Yet, this Episcopalian god liked self-deprecating humor; in one speech, he said, "In the corpo-rate pyramid, I'm the mummy."

Another client had no sense of humor, but he had excellent taste in hypocrisy. A self-made king of the futures markets, he wanted to be a sophisticated wit: the Noel Coward of the pork bellies' pit. I accommodated him with droll observations about the notorious frenzy of the markets. "Our method of trading combines elements of primal scream, aerobic dance and the battle of Hastings."

On one occasion, however, I had to cope with a speaker who had an identity crisis. Having heard a prominent businessman regale an audience with folksy anecdotes of a boy-hood in North Carolina, my client wanted a speech "just like that!" Unfortunately, reality was not particularly obliging. My client was a boychick from Bayonne, New Jersey. What exactly is the Yiddish word for *possum*? Since he wanted the absurd rather than the funny, I confronted him with the truth. I never got another assignment from him. I somehow sur-vived, but he has been reduced to using Dennis Rodman jokes.

The humor must be tailored to the speaker, but it also should be compatible with the audience. There may be a reason why Harvey Fierstein never appeared on "Hee Haw." Consider the composition and the character of your audience. Will your listeners find the humor in your remarks? There can be a fine line between humor and idiosyncrasy, and it is easy to stray. I have done it, as you are about to learn.

I was writing for a suave executive, and the humor reflected his preference for drawing room quips. The speech was on business management, and it mocked "the corporate hier-archy with more titles than *Burke's Peerage*." That line might have amused the staff of *The New Yorker*, but our audience was comprised of engineers. They did not get the joke, and I suspect that neither did you.

I must learn that not everyone watches *Masterpiece Theater*. Most people would not know that *Burke's Peerage* is the almanac and Yellow Pages of the British aristocracy. The book is nothing but lofty titles. I was comparing *Burke's Peerage* to the corporate hierarchy, where there seems to be a vice president for every occasion and excuse. The comparison is apt, but it is esoteric.

Unfortunately, the audience did not meet my standards of wit and erudition, and I was in no position to fire it. In fact, I failed the audience. There is a purpose to humor: communication. I had intended to make a droll indictment of corporate management. Perhaps I thought of the cleverest way to express the idea, but it was also the least intelligible. The audience deserved better.

As speakers and writers, we also must consider if the topic is suitable for humor. Would humor emphasize your ideas or sabotage them? Even good jokes can be inappropriate. If the audience expects a serious speech, a humorous tone could belie your message and credibility. A boring accountant is much more reassuring than a funny one. Indeed, the tactless joke or the flippant attitude can turn a speech into a suicide note.

History offers a famous example of that mistake. When on trial for impiety, Socrates ridiculed the ignorance and hypocrisy of his critics. Posterity admires his courage, but his audience did not. His defiance convicted him, and his mockery condemned him. Yes, Socrates was speaking the truth, but he might have chosen a more tactful manner of expressing it. One should never offend the audience, especially when it is a jury.

Having terrified you with the risks of humor, let me entice you with its rewards. Humor is the most irresistible form of communication. It has a contagious appeal that can win friends, arguments and elections. Can you recall a single joke by Walter Mondale or Michael Dukakis? Humor can be more than just a ploy for the audience's attention; it can be a sly but incisive expression of your ideas. Martin Luther certainly thought so. The founder of the Reformation was both a doctor of theology and a master of ridicule.

Luther could have expressed his beliefs in a scholarly Latin essay, but how many people would have understood it? The rebellious professor wanted the largest possible audience to know his opposition to the Church; so he wrote jokes in German. The humor was a broad and bawdy attack on the Church, and it delighted the public. His mockery expressed the popular resentment against an ostentatious and arrogant Church. The Ninety-Five Theses could be called the Ninety-Five Punchlines, a barrage of quips and insults aimed at the Pope. Luther lambasted the Pope as a spoiled rich kid who knew more about art than religion. The ridicule proved a most successful form of heresy. Furthermore, the humor was not lost in translation. Within a few years, the jokes and the Reformation had spread throughout Europe.

Luther used humor to convey and emphasize his ideas. His jokes were not irrelevant warm-ups for the sermon. They were integral to his text. Now, if humor can incite Reformation and a century of religious wars, think of how it can help you. Humor can illuminate and illustrate; it makes an insidiously good teacher. For example, the conflict between medicine and ethics is not a funny topic; yet I found that humor offered an enlightening perspective. If I may plagiarize myself, this example is from a speech that the Chairman of Baxter International gave at the Harvard Business School.

"The professional standards of medicine include a commitment to knowledge and research, intellectual principles that have continually challenged the prevailing ethics of their times. In 13th century Italy, the study of anatomy clashed with Christian values. If man were created in God's image, dissecting a corpse would seem clearly sacrilegious. The Church and the universities, however, reached a compromise on that matter. Physicians and medical students could dissect executed criminals, who evidently weren't going to look good on Judgment Day in any case."

Now, let us dissect the humor and the point of that example. Was I just flaunting my knowledge of history? Yes, I always do that, but sometimes there is a purpose. I was illustrating the clash between innovation and convention, and I could not resist the irony. The humor was not forced or obtrusive; it was the natural style of narration. How would you classify the humor? It certainly was not a belly laugh; I did not have an audience of blue-blazered MBAs rolling on the floor. You would not describe the example as a joke; it has to be told in the specific context of the speech. The humor is a matter of tone; the wit is in the phrasing.

Now, we must confront the fundamental question: how to be funny? Humor is quite similar to poetry. They both require the creative and succinct use of words. Meter and timing are the same thing. The wrong word, an extra syllable or misplaced emphasis could ruin a poem or a joke. Consider this classic line: "Take my wife . . . *please.*" Henny Youngman crafted a four-syllable joke that defies improvement. A poet could only aspire to such incisive eloquence. Indeed, humor may be more difficult than poetry. That was the opinion of T.S. Eliot, who admitted that he was not particularly funny. Eliot received the Nobel Prize for his poetry, but he wrote fan letters to Groucho Marx.

Humor demands originality. A stale joke will sabotage the speaker and the speech. Your speaker will be unnerved by the silence of a failed joke, and the trite humor will squander the attention and patience of the audience. If you hope to get fresh jokes from newsletters and websites, so does everyone else. You should write your own humor. Does that seem a daunting challenge? It shouldn't. You have the advantage of living in an absurd world.

Everyday we confront the elements of comedy. Turn on the news and get the daily chronicle of the shameless and the ridiculous. If you need further aggravation and bewilderment, just open your mail. You will find utility bills that defy explanation, offers for credit cards from your local barber college, and a proclamation that you have won millions of dollars from a fictitious sweepstakes. And who among us has been spared the most prevalent form of modern sadism: customer service! When you spend 15 minutes on hold, listening to an endless rendition of "Rhinestone Cowboy," you have to suspect that life was meant to be a satire.

Writing humor is a matter of observation. In an absurd world, the facts will speak for themselves and be self-incriminating. The speechwriter simply has to make the best use of the wry, the ironic and the ridiculous. So, a naked plumber walks into a bar . . . What happened next? It is a test of your talent and judgment on how to end the story and how best to use it. Does it belong in a speech, who should say it and to what audience? There are challenges and risks in humor, but there are also undeniable rewards. Humor can be your most effective means of communication, and it certainly is the most enjoyable.

PART 1

Articulating Vision
for Your Organization

CHAPTER 1

Visionary Speeches

"The last thing IBM needs is a vision," former Big Blue chairman Lou Gerstner once said. But in the next ten years, through dozens of speeches, Gerstner proceeded to demonstrate that IBM could not get along without a vision. Every organization needs a vision and a leader capable of articulating it. Employees look to leaders for only a few things: Invoking the imagination of the employees about the organization is perhaps the most important. There are few rules for doing so except to speak regularly, both formally and informally, about the organization. The speeches and remarks take many forms, but all the speeches

- Hold out high expectations
- Celebrate all that has been accomplished or confronted
- Focus on one or two specific points
- Use an inclusive, "we're in this together" voice
- Issue new challenges
- Call for a specific action or outcome
- Express confidence in the future
- Promise greater glories
- Offer a predictive, dreamlike quality
- Are upbeat in tone

Hope Is the Ability to Hear the Music of the Future

Tom Thompson, BellSouth

It's not easy to give a "futurist" speech. It's tempting to give your audiences a bunch of statistics and then extrapolate from those statistics. But few audiences like statistics. In this speech, by telecommunications executive Tom Thompson, VP of corporate and external affairs at BellSouth, the vision is light on statistics and long on stories. Filled with wit and jokes, the speech is a model of announcing a future that may not be obvious.

Scoping Document

Event:	Keynote remarks for second day of three-day computer conference
Theme:	Telecommunications in a Wired World
Place:	Las Vegas Convention Center, Las Vegas
Date:	November 12, 1999, 8:00 AM
Audience:	Approximately 2,000 telecom professionals, including BellSouth competitors
Length:	About 15 minutes, 1,380 words

Speech

I want to paint for you today a big picture of the information industry that not only includes the traditional telephone business, but also includes the Internet, wireless communications, and other slices of the telecommunications pie. Taken together, it may give us some real food for thought.

In so doing, I'm going to sound somewhat like a futurist.

Talking Points

Starting with a mixed metaphor ("painting a picture" and "food for thought") creates a vivid opening image.

Now, I don't want to sound like the futurist who back in the 1890s used scientific logic to say that New York City would be abandoned as unfit for habitation by the 1930s. His argument was based on projections of population growth.

Setting up a story to illustrate the difficulty of predicting the future.

He correctly estimated that New York's population would grow from 4 million to more than 7 million in 40 years. It was therefore obvious, he said, that the number of horses necessary to provide transportation for that many people would result in a public health hazard of incredible proportions, because there would be horse manure up to the third-floor windows everywhere in Manhattan.

Obviously, one can get into trouble by assuming that technology is frozen in time.

What is not "frozen" is the size of the telecommunications pie . . .

But what this does NOT show are the incredible growth opportunities all around the world.

Did you know that half the world's population—over two billion people on this planet—have never made a telephone call?

Provocative question.

Yet the economics of wireless technology and higher standards of living in developing countries are just the right ingredients to create sensational demand for wireless communications. It takes much less time to build out a cellular phone system than it does a regular landline telephone network, because there is no cable to bury underground or to hang from poles.

Explains international efforts.

That's why you're hearing about BellSouth and other companies bidding for cellular licenses in places like Peru, Brazil, and India.

And as soon as you create instantaneous communication like wireless technology affords, "distance" becomes irrelevant and people are linked together no matter where they may be geographically. That creates endless opportunities for commerce and a truly global society.

However that's NOT to minimize the outstanding growth opportunity alive in this country at this very moment. Forty-four million people in this country have cellular phones. Many of those are Internet users, and practically every one of them has at least one local telephone line and regular access to long distance service.

There are 60 million cable television households in this country, and in case you didn't know, cable television companies have the technology to offer phone service and Internet access, and you'll continue to see them entering those businesses.

If you see through my numbers, what I'm saying is that there is now at least an information-laden 40 to 60 million people in this country who have several different media at their disposal for information gathering and dissemination.

So all over the world, the race is clearly on between all kinds of technology firms to be the one-stop source of a consumer's communications needs. And certainly, my company, BellSouth, is a player in that race.

In fact, BellSouth's stated mission is "bringing people and information together." But while those exact words may not be on every technology company's annual report, that one-stop goal definitely is their motive.

Back to the domestic market.

By allying with the audience in interpreting the numbers, the speaker engages in a powerful way.

For those 40 to 60 million people who use several different types of communication, each one writes different checks each month to different providers. Does this make sense in a drive-thru society?

That's why the marketplace is telling the information industry, "Look. What I want is information. It doesn't really matter whether I get it over a wire or over the air. What does matter is who can get this information to me the most reliably, simply, quickly, at the lowest cost and on one bill?"

Beginning the visionary part of the speech.

Let me give you an illustration. Each of us probably has as many as half a dozen phone numbers assigned to us.

For example, my business card might look like this, with my office phone, my two cell phones, my pager (I have both a 1-800 and a local number), my fax machine, my home number, and my two e-mail addresses.

Helpful to actually hold up a business card, even if an image is projected on a screen.

Our business cards wind up looking like telephone directories!

The industry is feverishly anticipating this demand and responding to exactly this type of dilemma. A very recent example comes from MCI, who just a couple of weeks ago announced an offering to business customers that would link all their employees' telephones, cellular phones, voicemail, pagers and fax machines with ONE TELEPHONE NUMBER. That telephone number can even be set for easy recognition.

For example, my number might be 1-800-CALL-TOM. That number would be how you reach me no matter if I'm on a cell phone, a regular phone or whether you want to fax me.

Isn't it exciting to know you'll never be able to be alone again in your life?

Transition with a joke in the form of a question.

But seriously, everything from our national economy right down to our personal productivity depends on affordable, dependable access to information.

Our lives are sometimes like the guy who was driving a truck on a narrow two-lane road up the side of a steep mountain. He was backing up traffic even further because every few hundred yards he would stop, get out of the truck and beat the sides with a baseball bat. Finally one angry motorist behind him shouted "why are you stopping and beating your truck?" He shouted back, "I've got a one-ton truck with two tons of canaries inside. I have to keep at least half of 'em flying all the time."

To set up my "crystal ball" of the future, let's remember what Telecom 101 tells us about information. Basically, there are three types of information—voice, video and data. Historically, we know that telephone wires carried voice calls, big businesses used bigger wires to carry data between locations, and television used signals and coaxial cable to carry video.

Announces three issues to be discussed.

We're not quite to the place where, like in last year's Monday Night Football commercial, Hank Williams Junior offered to "let me fax you a beer." But we're close.

Here is my prediction: In the short term, you will see more mergers and acquisitions as today's firms gain the skills they need to offer more choices, and as they jockey for tomorrow's prime positions. In the long term, the telephone, the computer, the television, the pager, the fax machine, and the wireless

Prediction is part of most visionary speeches.

phone—will become one communications technology. It will have enormous potential to both enrich and simplify our lives.

Your communications system of tomorrow will be so different from today's that it will be hard to recognize . . .

Follows this statement with supporting examples.

Someday buying communications in pieces . . . will seem as strange as buying the pieces of a car and trying to put them together yourself.

If we can dream just a minute, can we envision that the revolution in telecommunications could, for example . . .

Visionary themes.

Curb pollution by letting many, maybe even most of us work from home?

These themes are articulated in crisp, bullet-point style.

Make access to information universal and thus spread democracy even to authoritarian countries?

Let us live anywhere we choose?

Bring world-class health care to remote areas?

Bring about, at long last, true education reform?

Of course it could!

Of course, these things are already beginning to happen.

The implications of information technology "convergence" for the 21st century are monumental and will involve every one of us. But my key message to you today is—do not be intimidated by it. Instead of being overwhelmed, look at it as an opportunity.

Look at the skills and talents you and your organization have, and then look at the tools you have to spread your product, service or ideas to a worldwide audience always thirsty for more information.

Here is a quotation that sums up how I believe we should respond to the massive but ultimately positive changes coming down the road. It's a redefinition of two familiar words. Here's how it goes.

"Hope is the ability to hear the music of the future. Faith is the courage to dance to it today."

Quotation from Peter Kuzmic, theologian and author.

I hope we've stirred up your imagination a bit today. Can we hear the first strains of the music of the future? If so, the challenge for all of us is to go and dance the night away . . . .

Stirring closing invoking the metaphor of music and dance.

3

We Have Met Our Threat, and It Is Us

Earnest W. Deavenport Jr., Eastman Chemical Company

"Terrorism Is Not Our Greatest Threat." That was the contention of retired Eastman Chemical Company CEO Earnest W. Deavenport, Jr., in an acceptance speech at the Society of Chemical Industry's 69th Chemical Industry Medical Award Dinner, October 16, 2001. The speechwriter's challenge here was threefold. First, the speech had to be in the context of the terrorist events of September 11. Second, Deavenport wanted a thought-provoking approach that went beyond the stereotyped sentiments that many people expected. Third, it was to be an after-dinner speech when audiences are reluctant to accept challenging topics. Says the speechwriter, Fletcher Dean, the resulting approach allows Deavenport to articulate a different view on terrorism and U.S. domestic policy. "As a result, it's a bit different from much of what we hear these days, which helped tremendously in keeping audience attention."

Scoping Document

Event:	Acceptance speech
Theme:	Post September 11, 2001 America
Place:	Society of Chemical Industry's 69th Chemical Industry Medical Award Dinner
Date:	October 16, 2001
Audience:	Approximately 500 chemical engineering professionals
Length:	About 12 minutes, 1,143 words

Speech

Many people don't realize that today is the birthday of Noah Webster. He's the man, of course, who gave us the first true American dictionary.

I mention that only because of how useful I thought it might be, especially to this group. Any one of you, for example, can go to Webster's dictionary and look

Talking Points

Uses topical introduction to make a point.

up the meanings to words and phrases you just don't hear that often anymore. Words like *profit . . . bull market . . . earnings growth*. Those are good American words that none of us have heard much of lately.

It reminds me of a story I heard about a Boston socialite who was out on the town one night and ran across one of her upper-crust lady friends. It seems the woman was engaged in what can best be called the world's oldest profession.

Naturally, the socialite was dumbfounded. And she wanted to know why her friend had stooped to this level. "My dear," her friend said, "it's either this or start dipping into capital."

Goes right into joke to set tone of speech.

These are difficult times. But this economic downturn was not totally unexpected. Even before Sept. 11, the signs pointed to some tough financial news.

First the bad news.

Many people—incorrectly I believe—point to Sept. 11 as the beginning of the unraveling. But I believe Sept. 11 was simply an accelerator.

Being here in New York, though, it's easy to see how that connection could be made. After all, the reminders surround us. They're on TV and the Internet. They're on the front page of every newspaper around the world. And certainly, Ground Zero is a constant, sobering reminder.

As a result, America's War on Terrorism—from Afghanistan to Iraq—seems to have become the nation's new battle cry. It's dominating talk at the dinner table just as surely as it's dominating the agenda in Washington.

But many of the problems the country faces today were here in the years before Sept. 11, and they'll still be here for many years afterward.

Despite all you hear about the impending crisis in Iraq and the continuing hunt for al Qaeda—and even despite what we hear from many politicians today—my firm belief is that terrorism is not the greatest threat to our country.

Hints at uplifting theme of speech.

True . . . terrorists have the potential to kill many innocent civilians. True . . . they have the potential to disrupt our lives. We've all experienced that. And it's true that they apparently have the wherewithal to continue as a thorn in our side for many years.

Anticipates the arguments of his critics and responds.

But terrorists will not topple this country. Nor do they need to. We're at risk of doing that ourselves. The greatest threat to our country doesn't come from outsiders, but from us.

This great experiment called America is at risk of imploding because of our inattention to the very things that have made us great.

Here is the speaker's main theme.

Once upon a time, this country had several advantages to its credit. We had vast, untapped natural resources. We had an educated populace. We touted scientific innovations like proud grandparents. We backed up our advantages with the vast power and superiority of America's business community. We ran our lives—and businesses—with a common set of moral values. And we prided ourselves as the true keepers of democracy in the free world.

Sets up the arguments the other side might muster and proceeds to demolish each one.

Which of those advantages can we still claim today? Natural resources? The most important one today is oil, and we certainly can't claim an advantage there.

A series of questions leads the audience to wait for the answers. Make sure the

An educated populace? Not if you look at the test scores of our high school students.

Scientific innovations? Many countries today could lay claim to making things cheaper, faster and better than us. Superior business climate? Not likely in the face of growing legal liability concerns from our courts and a growing anti-business slant from our legislators.

And who among us believes America has been true to its heritage of setting—and achieving—high moral standards, the very foundation of a civil society?

Which brings us to our claim as the keepers of democracy. That's the bottom line. Take away our other advantages and the very identity of our nation as a bastion of democracy is threatened.

What can we do about it? First, we can put our own house in order by focusing on those few things with the most potential. There are many things we could work on but I believe there are three in particular that need our immediate and committed attention.

The first is an overhaul of our K through 12 education system . . .

All of us—even those of you without kids in school now—have a tremendous stake in education. It's the minimum requirement to sustain our way of life. American businesses desperately need employees with higher skills. But more important, our democracy needs students able to think for themselves and become adult citizens intelligently involved in the issues of the day.

The founder of the University of Virginia—and our third president—Thomas Jefferson, put it best when

questions you ask are the ones the audience wants to have answered.

Powerful rhetorical question.

Visionary theme comes out here along with his prescriptions for a better future.

Frames the speech by announcing he will discuss three points.

The speaker follows this statement with an elaborate argument for improving education.

Pertinent quotation from the third president.

he said that "if a nation expects to be both ignorant and free, it expects what never was and never will be."

Related to this is the fact that our kids today—as well as some of our colleagues in corporate leadership roles— seem to have lost the one thing that helped create and characterize our nation: a well-defined moral compass. I'm talking basic family, moral and ethical values that are the basis of true citizenship in our country.

Transitions to a discussion of citizenship, most of which is omitted.

And by citizenship I mean involved, participatory citizenship . . .

Here's a quick test. Let me see by a show of hands how many of you voted in the 2000 election. That's a pretty high number. It's more than the average, which was just above 50 percent.

Challenging the audience like this is risky because it can alienate the audience.

The fact is, you're the core. But if you think you and your family represent mainstream America, let me encourage you to visit any hospital emergency room on a Saturday night. That's where you'll see how the other side lives. That's where the fringe is.

You and I have the power —indeed you and I have the obligation—to influence that for the better, to enlarge the core and bring in more participants from the fringe.

I mentioned earlier there were three urgent items we should work on. K–12 education was the first. Restoring a shared sense of values—a moral compass—was second. The last item we desperately need to address is the continuing assault on American businesses. In particular, we need to rein in product liability abuses and introduce true, lasting tort reform . . .

Repeats the promise of three points.

Now the third, and the audience expects, the final point. This helps the audience pace itself. The examples of legal reform are omitted.

As we continue to find our place in the greater global arena, my most ardent desire is that we Americans not forget the very things that made our democracy and our country strong. It's imperative that we not only rekindle the memory, but that we create fresh ways to sustain and grow it for tomorrow.

"Grow it for tomorrow" is a splendid phrase to conclude a speech with.

Our Role as Business Leaders: The Future Won't Wait

Jerry R. Junkins, Texas Instruments

Jerry R. Junkins is former chairman, president and chief executive officer of Texas Instruments, Inc. His remarks were presented to The Executives' Club of Chicago on September 22, 1995. This relatively lengthy speech calls on an elaborate organizational structure and numerous cues to make it work.

Scoping Document

Event:	The Executives' Club of Chicago
Theme:	The Future Won't Wait
Place:	Hilton Towers Hotel, Palace Ballroom, Chicago, Illinois
Date:	September 22, 1995
Audience:	Approximately 250 Chicago-based chief executives and senior managers
Length:	About 33 minutes, 3,277 words

Speech

My goal today is to get us all thinking together about the future.

It's a future that, as many of you know and are participating in, is based on some of the most powerful technologies the world has ever known.

But let me preface my remarks with a disclaimer: It's not my intent to regale you with tall technological tales . . . taken straight from the fast lane of the information superhighway. There are a lot of people in this audience who are more expert on that than I am.

What I would like to do is focus on our role as business leaders in bringing about the benefits that this

Talking Points

Direct opening is always appreciated.

Sets up the audience's relationship with the subject.

A disclaimer always gets attention. This one disarms the audience.

Focuses theme of presentation.

technological revolution is allowing to happen—
the benefits of a truly networked society . . . one
that releases the full promise of information
technologies.

Over the past decade, we've seen ample proof of
just how powerful these technologies can be—in
industry after industry. Automobile manufacturers.
Consumer products makers. Health care providers.
Retailers and distributors. All have learned to use
information technologies to get better . . . and
quicker . . . at responding to marketplace demands.

Audiences like examples. Note use of "we" for the first time.

In my judgment, the first 20 or 30 years of the information revolution did very little to change the way
we manage. I've likened it to automating the Big
Chief tablet: we didn't do much that was different
from the way we'd done it before.

Provocative statement. Another analogy possible here: paving the cowpaths.

But today's technologies have made it possible to
truly rethink the way we manage. The traditional
pyramids of command and control are starting to
crumble. New information systems have allowed us
to flatten our organizations—and re-engineer our
processes—not only on the plant floor, but throughout the enterprise.

"Pyramids" is a striking word.

Just as important—maybe even more so—is that
information technologies have revolutionized our
customer relationships. We're adding value in the
supply chain with electronic data interchange. We're
using networks and computerized order entry to
squeeze costs out of our distribution system . . . and
transforming distribution from a cost-center into a
strategic competitive advantage.

Future: theme of what lies ahead.

So, clearly, businesses understand the potential of
information technologies—and we're putting them

to work. But if we think we've already reaped the big benefits, you better think again. The really *radical* change is still ahead.

What do I mean by radical? In the 1980s, we talked about microprocessors inside personal computers that were operating at 10 million instructions per second. Today, the laptop computer that we've just introduced runs at 100 million instructions per second. And by the next decade, we'll see the same pattern of growth—running up to 300 or 400 million instructions per second, even in hand-held units.

The same sort of dynamics are also transforming the network. Today's copper cables can team up with fancy modems to deliver about 38,000 bits of data per second. We don't even know how much we can transmit through fiber. We're already approaching a billion bits per second—that's enough to transmit every issue of the *Wall Street Journal* ever published in the blink of an eye.

The convergence of computing power and networking technology will add up to enormous opportunities for business—much greater, I think, than any of us estimates today. Not only for companies like ours, which make and sell the technology . . . but also for the companies that buy it and put it to work.

Today, we're limited to sending voice, text and charts. Tomorrow, we'll be sending much *richer* messages— messages that incorporate pictures . . . sound . . . and video. And not just from one workstation to another . . . but from anyone, to anyone, anywhere in the world.

That's a far cry from e-mail. And it's not science fiction. The technology is literally around the corner.

I don't think technology is the issue. It's certainly not the only issue. In my judgment, it will be far outpaced by other things I want to talk with you about. It is clear that the bright promise of these incredible new technologies can be delayed—or even snuffed out—by any one of a number of killer issues.

Announces what the issue is not.

As business leaders, we can't afford to let that happen. That's why I welcome the opportunity to spend some time with you today. I believe we can—and we must—play an increasing role in the global community to unlock the full potential of these information technologies. Our leadership is crucial—because the barriers are extremely complex. They are interrelated. And they defy simple solutions.

What barriers am I talking about? Let me list just a few:

Audiences like lists, but only if the listed items are pertinent and logical.

- Trade protectionism and regulation
- The infrastructure gap
- Enforcement of intellectual property rules
- And a range of social policy issues like education and privacy protection.

If you examine these barriers in detail, it quickly becomes apparent why they have the power to short-circuit the future's bright promise.

Audience expects the speaker to address each of these issues in turn. Here the speaker enters into a contract with audience.

Let's talk about free trade. It seems self-evident that open markets are essential to the development of a truly networked society—a world where there's easy access to digital technologies . . . and where all the technologies can be linked according to accepted global standards.

Offers details about free trade.

But the reality falls far short of that ideal today, and it probably will tomorrow unless we make some changes. Instead of open markets and free trade, you encounter a hodge-podge of design standards and import barriers. Countries around the globe—from Germany . . . to Japan . . . to India . . . to Brazil— have put policies in place to protect local industries and limit foreign investment.

First issue. Offers details about protectionism.

These policies, we know, are short-sighted at best. But they continue to be put in place, and they pro-duce enormous inefficiencies in developed economies. Take Germany, for instance—where Byzantine work rules keep the telephone monopoly saddled with thousands of workers it doesn't need. As a result, the cost of basic telephone service is 2 or 3 times the rate people pay in the United States or the United Kingdom.

Gives example.

Maybe even more worrisome is when protectionist policies are fostered in developing economies, because they can cut these countries off from full participation in the global marketplace. Look to Brazil, for instance. In very recent times, stiff trade barriers stifled economic growth throughout the 1980s. TI was barred from bringing in the latest test equipment to test products we were manufacturing there, raising local prices as well as export prices.

A few years ago, many of Brazil's tariffs were reduced or removed—sparking a turnaround that produced a $10 billion trade surplus in 1994, and nearly 6 per-cent real economic growth. But, unfortunately, as has happened in the past, as consumer spending increased and imports grew, Brazil once again slapped tariffs in place and slowed its economy to a crawl.

Gives example.

There are, of course, some signs that leaders around the world are starting to recognize the need for change. Trade agreements like GATT and NAFTA are certainly a step in the right direction. But we've got a lot further to go—first, to include the many nations who are not parties to the existing treaties, and then, move a whole lot faster to implement the agreements we've already signed. There is still much work to be done.

How can we help keep the free-trade process moving forward?

Transition by asking question and then answering it.

First, all of us can help by stepping up our participation in trade organizations . . . on standards committees . . . and so on.

Maybe most important, we've got a big job ahead of us to counter the rhetoric of those who advocate sealing America's borders . . . and who fail to recognize that today's markets are truly global. We've got a big job to educate our political leaders— particularly our legislative leaders—as well as our own people and those in the communities where we live. And we *must* keep the pressure on our political leaders . . . and urge them to push ahead . . . despite the frustrations we and they will inevitably encounter along the way.

A second key issue we need to consider is what I'll call "bridging the infrastructure gap." In some quarters, this discussion revolves around universal access. In our rush to adopt new information technologies, the question is, are we creating an international society of technological "haves" and "have-nots"?

Second issue.

It's a fair question, especially when you consider the oft-quoted fact that about a third of the world's population has never used a telephone, let alone a computer or a fax machine. But it's not, in my judgment, the question many of the world's emerging countries are asking.

They're not worried about becoming information backwaters. They're wondering how they can turn their technological blank slate into a powerful strategic advantage.

And so, all of a sudden, you find that emerging areas like Latin America, some parts of Africa and Eastern Europe have become the fastest-growing cellular markets in the world. Over the next five years, wireless communications in these markets will grow at many times the rate of the developed countries.

Cellular systems make sense in undeveloped countries because it's cheaper to build radio towers than to string cable across the countryside. But the cellular users in these markets are now reaping some unintended benefits, too—like having a reliable communications system that doesn't tie them down to a single office or plant.

While you're thinking about the kind of advantage it must be to have a completely wireless view of the world, think about Vietnam. Vietnam has made a national commitment to install 300,000 new telephone lines a year over the next decade—all served by state-of-the-art fiber optic cable and digital switching.

More examples.

Or think about the opportunity in China. They plan to pour some $100 billion into telecom equipment— and add about 80 million new lines—by the year 2000. Here again, we're talking about digital fiber optic links . . . providing virtually unlimited transmission capacity between all of China's major cities and their trading partners.

These—and many other—emerging countries are taking advantage of the fact that they don't have billions of dollars invested in obsolete technology. And, maybe more important, they don't have the bureaucracy in place to inhibit development. They're finding that they can skip right past copper cable and analog switching systems . . . and build world-class information networks from scratch.

When you look at the infrastructure question from *that* perspective, you begin to wonder just who's on the wrong side of the gap.

Refers to infrastructure issue to keep audience on track.

And you're probably also starting to wonder who our global *competitors* will be three or four years from now. Chances are, the biggest threats won't come from Europe or Japan. We worry about competing against low-wage countries. Competing against low-wage countries that have raised their educational standards substantially and have the benefit of modern information technologies—that's something we really ought to worry about.

Anticipates question and then answers it. This tactic is useful as a way to pause the list of issues.

So how should we respond? Just recognizing the magnitude of the issue is a big step in the right direction. We have to take off the blinders that keep us from looking beyond our current trading partners and markets. We have to step up our investment in cutting-edge technologies, and make sure our own bureaucracy doesn't limit us.

Another question to lead to a discussion of the solution that the speaker supports.

And, further, many of us have the opportunity to influence what happens in countries around the world because of our presence there. We've got to increase our commitment to training our own people in a continuous learning environment. In short, we have to get a lot more comfortable with change

. . . or we could soon find that we've lost our lead to the economic juggernauts of tomorrow.

One part of a strategy for dealing with these emerging powerhouses . . . and with the rest of the global marketplace . . . must be to find more effective ways of protecting intellectual property rights. That's the third key issue we need to address.

Third issue.

That's a critical issue, in my view, and the reason is simple: if companies can't get a fair return on the resources they invest in new technologies, then they'll have no incentive to keep pushing the technology forward.

I speak from personal experience. TI spent 29 years trying to get the Japan Patent Office to recognize our fundamental patent on the integrated circuit— the basic building block of virtually all modern electronics.

Always good to recount personal experience.

We finally prevailed . . . only to have a Japanese district court in 1994 rule that our patent didn't cover products that are manufactured today. The court restricted the scope of the patent to the specific example that was used to explain the invention. It's as if we had been granted a patent on a *yellow* #2 pencil . . . only to be told that the patent doesn't apply if the pencil is painted *red*. The point is that if we use a narrow interpretation of this nature, it is difficult, if not impossible, to provide effective patent protection, particularly with respect to fundamental or pioneering technology.

Striking example that is easily remembered.

That's not the kind of environment that encourages leading technology companies to keep pushing the state-of-the-art forward. Nor is it an issue which is limited to the technology market in Japan. Intellectual property is at risk throughout the world . . . and across a wide range of industries.

In some countries, for example, as much as 95 percent of all the videocassettes sold are pirated. That means none of the people who actually created the value are getting paid for their efforts.

The same thing happens when software programs are passed around the office on a floppy disk. It may seem innocent enough . . . until you consider the hundreds or even thousands of hours that went into writing the source code. Without a fair method of compensation, what's the incentive for those programmers to continue to work?

Clearly, the existing laws are inadequate. Further, the agreements that are in place, like trade agreements, are too slow. We must work toward a new and totally different approach to intellectual property—one that addresses a wide range of markets and a wide range of issues such as ownership, royalties, entitlement and rewards.

Direct statement of belief backed up by opinions.

Here again, we in business must take a leadership role. We understand the business models. We've made the investments that are now at risk. So it's in our own best interests to play an active role in shaping and enforcing the next generation of intellectual property rules. If we don't find ways to level the playing field around the globe . . . and find them quickly . . . at a minimum it will slow down the opportunities our technology is generating; and in the worst case, it could well put us out of business.

There's one last set of issues I'd like to mention—and they involve a variety of social policy concerns that are created by today's information technologies.

Transition to closing. Audiences like these markers that the speech is not endless.

We've seen the two-edged nature of new technology in business, where advanced information systems

Examples of social policy concerns.

have created enormous opportunities—and created growth, and created thousands of jobs—for those who were prepared to change the way they work. But these same technologies have also caused a great deal of turmoil—they've literally put thousands out of work, by enabling businesses to automate many routine tasks.

Chances are, we can expect technology to have that same kind of disruptive impact on our social fabric, too.

We know, for example, that today's education system is deeply flawed. We live in a time when change is a constant companion . . . and when people will be asked to keep learning throughout their lives. But we're still relying on a model that assumes education stops at the age of 18 or 22.

Information technologies are challenging many of our other cherished assumptions, as well. Take privacy, for instance. In America, we value our privacy . . . and yet we cannot escape being lumped into dozens of databases.

Federal, state and local governments—they've all got our number . . . as do most of our favorite retailers and information services, too. Little by little, we're finding that otherwise helpful, and even essential, technologies are chipping away at our privacy. They're tipping the balance toward the potential for centralized control.

Nor is that the only potential privacy problem these new technologies create. Consider, for example, how easy it will be— and already is—for a competitor to spread malicious rumors about your products . . . and reach a worldwide audience . . . over the Internet.

It's tempting to say that these sorts of issues are not our concern . . . that matters like education and privacy can best be addressed by others who don't have quarterly earnings targets to meet. But I think that's short-sighted. We all have a stake in the future of the education system, if only because we depend on our schools to provide tomorrow's workforce and customer base.

The speaker here is speaking personally.

But beyond that, I think we may well find opportunity . . . if business makes a concerted effort to embrace social concerns. Imagine the market that could develop around new educational technologies, for example. What if, instead of teaching students about organ systems by dissecting frogs . . . we could challenge them to *design* a frog using computer-aided design software?

Ends by asking questions the audience is expected to take away from the speech.

Or, what kind of market could you build if you were the first to develop a device, or a method, that gave individuals or industries complete control over access to their personal information—and still allowed them complete access to the worldwide network?

More questions.

I don't mean to suggest that every issue boils down to a matter of dollars and cents. What I am saying is that we need to take an imaginative look at the problems our communities face and that these technologies can affect.

We can't keep turning to the usual suspects for answers. We need to look in the mirror instead . . . and start putting our vaunted problem-solving skills to work.

I said at the outset that my goal today was to start thinking a bit about the future. I hope I've made the

Transition to closing with the speaker hoping he made his case.

case that information technologies are changing our world—changing it in some ways that many have forecast, and in other ways we might not expect.

Without a doubt, these technologies will touch off an enormous shift in our economic, social and political structures. And they promise enormous benefits, too—chief among them, the opportunity to live and work in a world that knows no boundaries.

Conclusion by restating the premise.

The question is, will we be ready—as a society and as a nation—to clear the hurdles we will inevitably face? Will we be prepared to tackle complicated issues, the likes of which the world has never seen?

Challenge to the audience.

Not without our best minds . . . and not without our most capable leaders.

We must begin today . . . to broaden our view beyond our own profit performance and market share and local issues. We can start, by educating ourselves and our people about the issues I've mentioned here this afternoon.

Reminds audience of challenge.

And then, we have to act. It's up to us to support the critical policy issues—like intellectual property protection and global technology standards.

Restates some of the key issues discussed in the speech.

It's up to us . . . to counter misleading rhetoric about free trade . . . with well-reasoned, high-profile responses that speak to the realities of a global marketplace.

It's up to us . . . to bring the benefits of information technology not only to our companies, but also to America's communities and schools . . . so that our infrastructure can become and remain the equal of any in the world.

Concludes with a dramatic series of themes all beginning with the same phrase.

It's up to us . . . to be sensitive and responsive to the social implications of our technology . . . and to be imaginative in our attempts to address those concerns.

It's up to us . . . to do these things . . . and do them all *at once* because the future won't wait. The technologies are here. They're already stirring the pot.

Our challenge is not so much to harness those technologies . . . as it is to unlock their potential.

It certainly won't be easy. But with the sustained focus of business leaders—with the commitment of all of us—I believe that we *can* realize the full promise of a networked society: The promise that it will dramatically improve the quality of life for the entire world.

Ends on hopeful note.

Have Fun: Making Good Decisions in Bad Times

Harry C. Stonecipher, Boeing

The Boeing Company was in transition when then president and CEO Harry C. Stonecipher addressed the Young Entrepreneurs Organization (YEO) Annual Conference. The company had relocated its headquarters from Seattle to Chicago. Within 25 days of delivering this speech, the events of September 11, 2001 would plunge the company into deeper turmoil. The signs of warning were everywhere. After 10 years of expanding economy, the stock market was dropping and the U.S. aerospace industry was losing market share to foreign competitors. This speech is prescient for its determination to confront the unknown.

Scoping Document

Event:	Young Entrepreneurs Organization (YEO) Annual Conference
Theme:	Managing in Uncertain Times
Place:	Grand Hyatt Hotel, Seattle, Washington, Elliott Room
Date:	August 17, 2001
Audience:	Approximately 400 members of YEO. (Most executives are under 40 years of age.)
Length:	About 17 minutes, 1,509 words

Speech	Talking Points
"Optimism is high moral courage."	*Starting with a quotation is a sound rhetorical decision if you follow it up and, ideally, conclude with the theme it introduces.*
So said Ernest Shackleton, the great polar explorer, and a personal hero of mine.	
Shackleton planned to cross the Antarctic continent on foot. However, after battling through thousands of miles of floating ice, his ship, the *Endurance*,	*Introduces Shackleton to those who do not know his career. This can be tricky, as you*

became locked in an ice pack and then crushed. Casting tents on the ice, the 27 men in Shackleton's party subsisted on a diet of penguins, dogs and seals from January of 1915 through April of 1916.

threaten to bore people who know the facts.

Under Shackleton's leadership, every man survived— not only in good health, but in good spirits as well. Remarkably, eight members of the expedition rejoined Shackleton on another Antarctic adventure a few years later. One of them called Shackleton "the greatest leader that ever came on God's earth, bar none."

Bold statement. The speech will now support the statement.

When he spoke of optimism as high moral courage, I believe that Shackleton was thinking of three kinds of optimism.

Announces he will describe three types of optimism. It might be good to list them here and then review them one by one.

First, there is the optimism that allows a person to dream an impossible dream or to pursue an improbable goal. All of you exemplify that kind of optimism. You would not have started businesses of your own without it.

First type of optimism. Note speaker's use of "you" to address audience.

As I see it, optimism as high moral courage also involves a willingness and determination to deal with great difficulties. Still further, it involves the capacity to radiate confidence. In difficult times, you need the kind of optimism that rubs off on others. As Napoleon said, "a leader is a dealer in hope."

Napoleon quotation.

I expect that some of you have already been tested in the second and the third elements of optimism.

Transition to the second and third types of optimism.

How many of you have experienced a downturn in the last year? How many of you have friends or competitors that have faced declining demand or falling prices for the first time? Have they maintained a capacity for bold and decisive action?

Asks a series of questions to set up the discussion he wants to have.

According to an ancient curse, whom the gods would destroy, they first punish with 20 years of success. Without a doubt, long success usually leads to complacency. And when growth comes to be taken for granted, it covers up a multitude of sins—inefficiencies, bad business practices and a certain carelessness or lack of foresight.

Follows with a series of stories and case histories (omitted here for reasons of space).

Now, the United States has enjoyed two decades of almost uninterrupted growth, led by the extraordinary performance of a multitude of smaller companies—with the most visible being those in high tech industries such as computers and telecommunications.

Let me give you my opinion . . . and this is the opinion of a capitalist war-horse of the old school—one who has carried the banner for large corporations into many a campaign. Regardless of Etoys, Kozmo, Webvan and other dot.coms that have fallen by the wayside, I am convinced that we are just at the beginning, and not at the end, of a golden age for entrepreneurship.

It's clear that he's offering an opinion.

The true wellspring of capitalism has always been the creation of new businesses. And there has never been a better time for starting your own business than right now. Today anyone can buy a computer for $800 that has more power than the mainframes of 40 years ago.

Follows with some personal stories about his own career.

I can assure you that big companies today are keenly aware of the need to stimulate risk taking, entrepreneurship and unconventional thinking within their own organizations. At Boeing, we have set up a $200 million in-house venture capital firm. It is there to encourage people to come forward with new ideas for starting businesses.

Now speaks more authoritatively.

What are some of the secrets to making the right decisions in hard times? Here, then, are some of the things that I have learned in more than 30 years in corporate management. During this time, I have been personally involved as CEO or president in three major corporate turnarounds. There is nothing particularly original about any of my five rules. I believe that Shackleton's extraordinary grace under pressure teaches the same lessons. So I will take the liberty of speaking for him as well as for myself.

Rule #1—Do not tolerate complacency at any time. Complacency is the worst of dangers because it is the one danger that obscures all of the others. Soon after they abandoned ship and pitched tents on the ice, Shackleton overheard two men ordering tea from the cook. One wanted his tea strong, the other weak. Shackleton was appalled that they could be concerned with trifles at such a time. To remind them of the gravity of their situation, he immediately cut the food allowance for all hands to a mere 9.5 ounces per day. Feeling that he had made his point regarding the seriousness of their situation, he rescinded this order a few days later.

Rule #2—Change the people, or change the people. Shackleton had no choice but to work with the crew with which he began. Knowing of the deadly consequences of internal dissension on earlier polar expeditions, he was rightly obsessed with the need for maintaining unity of command. He kept the few malcontents close to him—inside his own tent or his own boat—to contain their effect upon the others and to try to win them over.

Whenever I have joined a new company in a leadership position, I have always started with the attitude that every existing member of senior management

Transition by asking a question.

Back to Shackleton. Introduces five rules he will talk about in the balance of the speech.

First rule.

"For all hands" is a rhetorical device called synecdoche. For example, "All hands on deck" or "Lend me your ears."

Second rule.

should have a fair chance to prove his or her worth as part of a high-spirited and unified team. But I have always been prepared to change the people who cannot or will not change, or who cannot or will not act as team players.

Rule #3—Don't try to please everyone. To do so is to confuse popularity with leadership. Though he sought out advice, Shackleton made final decisions on his own. As he wrote in one of his two books, "Leadership is a fine thing, but it has its penalties. And the greatest penalty is loneliness."

Third rule.

Shackleton quote.

Rule #4—Maintain a clear-eyed view of reality, no matter how unpleasantly it may differ from what you expect, and be prepared to alter your plans and make new ones without delay or regret. This seems obvious, except that it is so often ignored in the behavior of companies and people alike. This comes, I think, from a fear of making any kind of decision until all of the facts are in, by which time it may be too late to act. Looking back on the key decisions that you have made in your life, how many times have you wished that you waited another six months to make this or that decision?

Fourth rule.

But plans were never just plans for Shackleton—to be filed away and forgotten. When the time came for action, he never hesitated. This was best illustrated in the final descent from the mountain that he and two members of his crew had crossed on their way to being rescued. Late in the day, they came to the edge of a steep crevasse. Convinced that the alternative would be death by freezing, Shackleton made a quick decision that stunned the other men. At his insistence, they linked legs and pushed off from a sitting position, descending like three tobogganers without a toboggan. In a wild, accelerating rush, they

What a wonderful story! Audiences need such stories.

plunged down more than 2,000 feet in about a minute and half. Coming to an abrupt halt in a snowbank, they broke out laughing uncontrollably. A terrifying prospect had turned into a breathtaking triumph, thanks to what was literally a seat-of-the-pants decision.

Rule #5—Have fun; it's an important part of being alive, and it can only help you succeed in whatever you are doing. I won't belabor you with Shackleton stories here, except to say that the diaries of all the crew members who kept them attest to the high spirits and high morale that prevailed almost throughout their two-year ordeal. Optimism was a great part of the bond that held them together, and that optimism did, indeed, amount to true moral courage.

Fifth rule.

I believe very strongly that business as a profession should be exciting and fun as well as rewarding in a financial sense. Since life is short, why not enjoy what you are doing? I give the rise of entrepreneurship a lot of credit for bringing a renewed sense of exhilaration to the art and science of business. Even in big corporations people are learning to have fun and to relish the challenge of forging coherent, high-performance teams out of the diverse elements of which they are made.

If optimism is not a part of the makeup of any business—big or small, young or old—a key element is missing.

In closing, I am not going to offer you the wish of smooth sailing in your future endeavors. Better than that, I would like to wish you the fortitude and foresight to both endure and prosper—not just in good times, but in hard times as well.

Gentle conclusion.

6

No One Reads Tomorrow's *Wall Street Journal* Today

Craig Howe

The challenge: to acquaint an audience of well-heeled executives with the firm's investment philosophy, its methodology, and the market's opportunities. The speech starts by referring to an occasion shared by many in the audience, the frenzied shoppers converging on the annual Brooks Brothers post-Christmas sale. In this speech, the firm's investing philosophy is entertainingly presented.

Scoping Document

Event:	Individual Investors' Conference
Theme:	Investing Strategies for the 1990s
Place:	Washington, D.C.
Date:	December 27, 1991
Audience:	Approximately 500 individual investors looking for investment tips
Length:	About 7 minutes, 680 words

Speech

December 27th is always a depressing day for me. This is the day Brooks Brothers begins its Annual Post-Christmas Sale.

Have any of you been there? Go ahead, raise your hands. How many of you have been to the first day of a Brooks Brothers Christmas Sale? Good, you will know what I am talking about.

Picture the scene with me. As you enter the store through those 16-foot tall, wooden doors from the Madison Avenue entrance, your eyes immediately see

Talking Points

Attention getting opening juxtaposed with a vivid image.

Asking for a show of hands builds community in an audience.

Don't leave audience members out. The speaker describes what he is referring to for the benefit

well-tailored men and women, standing two and three deep around the 15-foot-square tie counter.

of those who don't know about the Brooks Brothers sale.

These people, primarily men, are titans of their chosen professions, our economy's elite. They are successful, powerful, and yes, prime candidates for the investment services we offer at Fred A. Jones.

The depressing part of the scene is these people are not comporting themselves in a quote, gentlemanly, unquote fashion. Like pigs at a feeding trough, these value-wise individuals call upon blocking skills unused since their glory days on high school football fields to grab for their favorite regimental tie, which that morning was marked down a mere five bucks from its normal $40.00 selling price.

Delivers the promise of the opening line.

Now, I have nothing against saving money. What makes this scene so depressing to me—so depressing I cannot even summon the strength to enter the frenzy—is a simple observation . . .Wall Street is the only merchant I know who puts its goods on sale and no one shows up.

By now the audience is wondering what all this has to do with investing. The speaker is about to make the connection.

Marshall McLuhan tells us people march forward, looking backward. In the case of investors, they do not look back far enough. Investors tend to overpay for certainty. In doing so, they rob themselves of the opportunity for exceptional stock and bond market performance.

Invoking famous philosopher.

At Fred A. Jones we premise our investment philosophy on the fact that stocks and bonds often sell for their intrinsic long-term value. As investors, we naturally overpay for certainty. We also overcompensate for risk. We react in emotional ways to current events rather than examining these times under the rational microscope of long-term value.

Here's the main point of the speech. Details and examples omitted.

At Fred A. Jones & Co., we seek to exploit these distortions by applying intensive research, absolutely enforcing buy and sell discipline and maintaining a long-term focus.

Few people like to plan. When markets are rising, it seems unnecessary. As they fall, it seems futile. Yet, investment planning remains the route to optimizing your investment productivity—getting the most from your investments. It is the cornerstone of our management philosophy.

If you have not done it, begin today. Whether your goals are to provide additional income to live on, protect your estate or to assure your lifestyle is truly within your means. We encourage all clients to take advantage of this service—provided free of charge—at least once biannually. More often, if and as your circumstances change.

Four questions inevitably asked during beginning investment planning sessions are (1) Do I have enough? (2) Will I have enough? (3) How do I get started defining the best investment course? And—the most common question of all—(4) Can I do better?

Sound answers recognize some fundamental realities. Lifetimes are longer and so are retirements. Inflation has a powerful impact on long-term purchasing power.

Discretionary spending patterns and lifestyle requirements vary. Too much money in CDs or money markets compromises productivity. Stocks are the only asset class to meaningfully outperform inflation in the end.

The benefit the company offers.

Unstated invitation to audience members to test their behavior against the statement. Much preferred in such cases to asking for a show of hands, which many people would consider intrusive.

Directly engages audience.

Effective technique is to ask a handful of questions, which then serves to organize the main body of the speech.

The speaker refers to projected slides in discussing some figures.

The solution is a carefully selected portfolio of undervalued stocks and bonds, tailored to meet your investment objectives, and more importantly, your risk tolerance.

The portfolio should include enough growth to offset inflation, enough income to meet your current and future needs and enough diversity to insure asset growth.

Begin today. No one reads tomorrow's *Wall Street Journal* today. Unless you are very lucky, you will not time the end of the current correction.

Never in our history have we expected greater stock market returns than we do today.

The message I want to leave with all you tie buyers is, "The merchandise is on sale."

Conclusion. The speech might have included a bid for action, what the speaker would like the audience to do with the information it has just received.

Direct invitation.

Transition to conclusion. The wording to the all important conclusion must be packaged right. This is a bit off. Better: "Tie buyers, here's the one message I want to leave you with: "the merchandise is on sale."

CHAPTER 2

Motivational Speeches

Motivational speeches can be easy because people really want to be motivated. The hard part about delivering a message that they can believe is that you have to believe it, too. Effective motivational speeches all

- Stay upbeat—express appreciation for what the group has already accomplished
- Focus on a single objective and make only one primary point
- Are clear and direct—even about negatives
- Are inclusive—take a "we're in this together" tone of voice
- Imagine possibilities and illustrates them with concrete stories or anecdotes
- Offer a bid for action—calls for a specific set of behaviors
- Avoid generalities and fluff—audiences don't leave such speeches thinking, "What did he say?"

The following speeches and remarks all attempt to exhort the employees to take on renewed efforts. These are motivational speeches in the best sense of the term. Yet they are also speeches of appreciation and vision.

Americans Are Winners, Not Whiners

Jack Welch, General Electric

Jack Welch, now retired as chairman and chief executive officer of General Electric Company, is generally regarded as one of the best CEOs in history. In this 1992 speech, Welch's nemesis is bureaucracy. He offers readers much wisdom in how to accept an award. The secret? Accept the award on behalf of the company, talk grand vision, identify the challenges, register a bit of outrage, and offer some prescriptive advice.

Scoping Document

Event:	New England Council
Theme:	Private Sector New Englander of the Year Award
Place:	Boston, Massachusetts
Date:	November 11, 1992
Audience:	New England Council members
Length:	About 12 minutes, 1,236 words

Speech

I will accept this award gratefully, trying to use my best New England accent on behalf of the 25,000 GE employees from Bangor to Pittsfield to Warwick, who compete fiercely around the globe and have made our business—jet engines to electrical equipment to financial services to plastics—world leaders.

I have a view, based on the performance of our businesses and what I see around the world, that makes it difficult for me to share much of the pessimism about our economy and our country that seems to be a by-product of presidential campaigns.

I would not for a moment minimize some of the problems we face: the economy in New England,

Talking Points

Welch accepts the award on behalf of the team. Naming specific places locates the speech and creates a connection with those who identify with those communities. The downside is that some people may feel left out.

Identifies the problem: the deficit.

and nationally, the most significant and serious being the deficit. I think America owes a debt of gratitude to Senator Warren Rudman for focusing his energy and leadership on this classic "NIMBY"—"Not In My Backyard"—issue; one we all love to deplore, and one we all want someone else to fix.

But, for my part this evening, I'll be focusing on the half-full view of the glass. On a country with leaner, more productive companies forged by the restructuring of the last decade. A country with the world's best, most productive workforce and a country with enormous opportunities for nearly limitless growth and prosperity.

But then takes a hopeful attitude.

Now, no recession can be minimized if you are one of its statistics—particularly its unemployment statistics—but the rueful paradox for Mr. Bush was that the most significant statistic in his loss was probably unemployment, which, last Tuesday, was at the exact same level it was when the incumbent Ronald Reagan won a landslide victory in 1984.

Adds historical context.

But look at the positive signs that somehow got lost in the gloom: The great thief inflation has been stopped cold. Interest rates are the lowest in memory for most Americans. And exports. Exports have been growing, not declining, an average of 11 percent per year over the past five years. We are the largest exporter in the world, and we have the world's most productive economy.

I find it very difficult to look at the numbers and still see a glass half-empty—or even a broken glass—which is the view of some of the more depressed pundits.

Staying with the hope.

Over the last six months, have we heard any discussion of Europe, Mexico or Asia that was not shaded

Locates the speech in time and asks a series of questions.

in terms of threats to our markets, our standard of living? How much discussion of North American Free Trade have we seen that did not quickly focus on possible American job loss or the possibility of increased pollution?

What I see in Asia reminds me of what the post-war years of America must have been like—boundless growth, pent-up demand, optimism and opportunity. These nations have economies growing from 6 percent to 12 percent a year. The skies above their cities are a thicket of cranes. They need infrastructure, health care, technology—just what we have to offer. They like and respect America and want to work with Americans. What an opportunity for all of us!

Locates the speech in place: Asia, Mexico.

Visit Mexico and see a reborn economy that is ridding itself of corruption and bureaucracy. Mexico has, in President Salinas, arguably the most dynamic and transformational leader in the world. This is a nation leaping out of the Third World, one that will be importing $115 billion worth of goods a year by the year 2000. A nation with huge market opportunities closer to us in Boston tonight than is Los Angeles. And what do we focus on? Not on that growth, but on U.S. job loss claims that are simply untrue and dire predictions about pollution growth in Mexico that are whimsical and illogical.

Registers bit of outrage.

Sam Walton was an authentic American hero, certainly one of mine. But for one group of folks he has been nothing but trouble: those managers of mature businesses, of whatever size, whose standby excuse for stagnation is that their markets are mature, and therefore it's all beyond their control. What Sam Walton did was to go into one of the most mature industries of all and find a way to grow, grow, grow double-digit, month-after-month,

Locates the speech by hero.

year-after-year. He did it by innovation, customer focus and, above all, speed.

Speed is everything. It is the indispensable ingredient in competitiveness. Speed keeps businesses—and people—young. It's addictive, and it's a profoundly American taste we need to cultivate.

Companies and countries seem to follow predictable life cycles. In their infancy, new businesses are gripped by a shared urgency and breathless need to get to the marketplace. Some of the most exciting and memorable times of my life will always be those frantic days as part of a team trying to grow a plastics business out of Pittsfield. Bureaucracy simply can't get a foothold in an environment like that, the way ice can't form in a fast-moving stream. But as institutions prosper and get more comfortable, the priority begins to shift gradually from speed to control; from leading to managing; from winning to conserving what has been won; from serving the customer to serving the bureaucracy.

Transition to his main point: that companies and countries follow similar patterns.

We begin to erect layers of management to smooth decision-making and control all that growth, and all it does is slow us down. We put barriers between the functions of our business, which creates turf and fiefdoms; we blur our communications with businesses and jargon and allow the bureaucracy to get a toehold, then a foothold, and finally a stranglehold.

Everyone can relate to the problems of bureaucracy.

People say that now that the Soviet Union is out of business we have no more truly dangerous enemies. They're wrong. The Soviets couldn't beat us, but economically, the bureaucracy and bureaucrats still can.

The way to harness the power of these people is not to protect them, not to sit on them, but to turn them loose, let them go—get the management layers off

Now, having laid the foundation, Welch begins the prescriptive part of the speech.

their backs, the bureaucratic shackles off their feet and the functional barriers out of their way.

"Boundaryless" is the big clumsy word we use at GE and, whether in a company or in a society, it means engaging every mind on every problem, leaving no one out, weighing no one's ideas heavier because of the color of their collar or their skin, their gender, their nationality, or whatever.

Introduces some memorable jargon.

We find again and again that every barrier that divides us, between engineering and manufacturing, between us and suppliers or us and customers, between the preconceived view we have of Jakarta or Shanghai and the view we know of Boston or Des Moines, between genders, between races, every barrier—serious or silly—is a speed bump that slows us down and deprives us of the quickness we must have to capture the opportunity that is out there in abundance.

Note the use of "We" as a device to build a bridge to the audience.

This isn't theory. To be parochial for just a second, at GE we have grown our productivity 5+ percent a year right through the recession by beginning to make real a vision of a company where every mind is engaged.

Since everyone else will be handing out gratuitous advice to President-elect Clinton, I guess I can too: Americans are winners by nature, not whiners. Don't baby or patronize them or try to protect them. Appeal to their competitiveness, challenge them to break the barriers that separate and slow them down. Keep the bureaucrats and industrial policy types away from their enterprises, let them go—and watch what happens.

No one who has done that has ever been disappointed.

It's risky closing a conclusion with a negative, but here it adds a dramatic conclusion.

The Elephant in the Room: Responding to Being Passed Over

Tom Seip, Charles Schwab

In the executive ranks of most organizations, being passed over for a top job is usually handled in private, with a discrete resignation, and an announcement that the executive is pursuing personal interests. But the situation can also be used as a leadership learning opportunity.

By all accounts, Tom Seip, a former top executive at Charles Schwab & Company, was in line to become president of the brokerage subsidiary of Charles Schwab Corporation, the largest discount brokerage in the country. But then he received the devastating news that he was being passed over in favor of an outsider. By convention in most of corporate America, the only response would be to resign on the spot. But at Schwab a different corporate culture prevails. While Seip considered resigning, he not only changed his mind but sought an opportunity to explain his decision. He got his chance on October 16, 1997, when Tom Seip addressed the Charles Schwab senior management team. It was a remarkable speech in its level of personal detail, private anguish, and soaring demonstration of loyalty to the values that Schwab represented.

Scoping Document

Event:	Internal management meeting of Charles Schwab executives
Theme:	Company promotions
Place:	Charles Schwab headquarters, San Francisco, California
Date:	October 16, 1997
Audience:	Approximately 15 members of the Charles Schwab executive committee
Length:	About 15 minutes, 1,600 words

Speech

Two weeks ago, Dave asked me if I would speak to the group this morning, and frankly, I was surprised. It just had never occurred to me, but then we talked

Talking Points

Recounts origin of this most unusual speech. David Pottruck is CEO of the parent company.

a bit about potential elephants in the room during this meeting. For those of you who are new [to Schwab] we refer to "the elephant in the room" as the unasked, unanswered question on everyone's mind. In this case, perhaps there are some elephants in the room.

Announces theme of elephant in the room.

We've been talking about our challenges and opportunities for the last two days, and I think by now we all agree we needed some changes. That said, I would not for one moment want you to believe that I didn't want the job [of president of the brokerage subsidiary]. I did. I thought about it a lot, and I was terribly disappointed when I did not get the job. I was at first angry, of course, and because I was raised, like you were, to put tremendous value on where I was positioned in the hierarchy, it was a fairly significant blow to my self-esteem. And to the degree my identity is linked to my job, the answer to the question, "Who am I?" in this case comes back very quickly, "You are not the president." And so now what?

Very frank that he is disappointed at not getting the job.

Emphasizes community and teamwork.

Series of questions frames the discussion to come.

And I had to deal with that; not only for myself, but for my wife and family. There was the issue of how all of you would perceive me. That, by the way, was the biggest hurdle. In a sense, I felt I had somehow let you all down, and that this was one glaring sign of it that I could never recover from. That idea was nearly unbearable. There was a part of me that just wanted to disappear.

But I didn't. And I wanted you all to know why.

After all, we are all at a very high level of achievement. There are few people in this room who could not land another job in the timeframe they wanted, in the place they wanted, at roughly the pay they wanted. I'm no exception. Also, given the success we all have enjoyed in the last 15 years I've been here, I suppose I could have simply retired.

So the decisions were to stay or go, retire or find another job.

Let's take retirement first. When I first learned of my proposed role in the reorganization, I called a valued friend. He is a neighbor of mine and has remained a trusted friend and advisor. His response to my question about retirement was short, "What are you going to tell Parker?" he said.

Articulates three choices, each of which will be discussed.

Not many of you know I have two sons. Parker, at 15, is the elder. He is also a learning-differenced kid. Unlike me, and most if not all of you, school is for him a battle. Very hard work . . . every day . . . and then there is homework . . .

Not afraid to get personal.

So, we work very hard to instill in him the value of hard work. That is the norm, not the exception. And I try to model that behavior. Given that, how could I suddenly sleep in, work on my golf game three or four days a week, and spend my afternoons in my workshop trying to perfect the American cherry high-boy chest of drawers? Well, I couldn't. So retirement was out.

Dismisses option 1.

But while the decision not to retire was pretty easy, the process of deciding to stay here versus working elsewhere was not easy. It was, however, once again a chance to grow a little. And I am a growth junkie. Growth means change and adventure, and of course, the phrase, "growing pains" was not coined without cause . . . growth is usually painful, and absolutely essential to life. This has been a hallmark of my career, and I believe of my personal life, for more

Option 2.

than 45 years. And those ideas about growth were predominant in my thinking about staying or leaving Schwab. Here is just some of my thinking.

First: When we get to the point that we are in our chosen field . . . and this really goes for everyone in the room, we just simply have to learn to cope with what we might think of as career setbacks. I needed to not just understand, but really experience, the value of commitment and loyalty to the mission of the company and to all of you, and to see how far that commitment went beyond my own particular disappointment.

Involves the audience by referring to the team and by using "we" throughout.

Now that might sound like B.S. but it isn't, at least not for me. Understand that I'm not saying that if the headhunters call, and they will, that I won't listen. I'm still working through whether or not I need to be president of a company. And if I decide that I do, I will leave. But I really believe at our level in the organization, we should be expected to carry the mission of the company inside of us . . . at a gut level . . . in fact, it should be part of the requirement to be an officer of the company.

Along with that responsibility comes the requirement to recruit peers who can compete with us, people who are really good . . . and who can be better than we are. I have always preached this and practiced it. But of course, this means that we have to face the inevitability that our subordinates will become our peers, and our peers will become our bosses. But there is a payoff. It also means that we can take pride in those people rising to be our peers in the organization. This is just part of the biology of a good organization, and I think it is part of the DNA of a good leader.

Executives pay lip service to the notion that they should hire people better than they are. Seip actually lives it.

I had to really go through some questions and answer them truthfully. And the first question was, "What are the right questions?" Here were some of the questions that I came up with:

Effective use of the technique to ask yourself questions and answer them.

1. Do I believe in the mission of the company? Answer: of course.
2. How does the fact that you didn't get this job affect commitment to the mission of the company? Answer: not at all.
3. Is there any place else in the world, other than starting your own company, where you could express that commitment? Answer: probably not.
4. Do I believe in the strategy? Answer: I helped fashion it.
5. Is there any group of people that you would rather be with, leading and following . . . with all of the foibles and all the successes? Can you imagine having the kind of long-standing and committed relationships in another environment? Answer: of course not.
6. Do you respect the new person you are going to be working for? The answer: absolutely.

Most effective is when the questions are the same as the audience might be expected to ask you.

So then, for me, the only reason to leave would be petulance . . . because I didn't get to play the position I wanted to play. And then I asked, "How am I going to explain this to Jake, my 12-year-old son . . . who is a starting halfback on his middle school soccer team, but who wants to play center forward because there is more glory there? And who talks about quitting the team because the coach won't play him there . . . that I quit the team because I didn't get to be starting center forward? I had no answer to that . . . and I couldn't find one.

Analogy to son's sports team is devastating in its effectiveness.

To have to answer the question years from now . . . to my son or to anyone else . . . when someone asked me why I left Schwab . . . to answer that it was because my ego was injured . . . that was totally unacceptable to me.

So I decided that I wanted to stay. But there was a final set of questions about whether I should stay. The moral issue about whether or not it was right to continue taking a paycheck from the shareholders. This was framed in stark relief when one of the executives in this room rolled into my office a couple of weeks ago and said he'd heard he was going to be working with me again. I asked how he felt about that and he answered with a question of his own: "Are you here or are you 'in transition'?" And, we all know what he meant. Was I excited? Did I have the energy? Or, would I just be going through the motions?

Option 3.

More tough questions.

In the final analysis, the decision was really pretty easy. The hard part was really coming to grips with growing up as a leader, to decide not to pout and retreat, but to constructively go forward, to go on to the next challenge and continue to build on what we have here that is so very, very special.

So I am still playing, better than ever I hope, in the right industry, where I can actually provide something that people need, in the right company, where we are truly serving, not selling, and with the right group of people . . . all of you and the thousands who are not here. As Chuck said . . . it's nice to go to work every day feeling like you are doing something important . . . fundamentally to help people . . . with people you care about. And then, of course, there is the world domination part!

To Schwab people, chairman of the board Charles R. Schwab is always "Chuck."

Truthfully, it doesn't get a whole lot better.

Thesis statement used as conclusion.

Congratulations on a Job Well Done

Dr. Shirley Ann Jackson, U.S. Nuclear Regulatory Commission

This speech by Dr. Shirley Ann Jackson, former chairman of the U.S. Nuclear Regulatory Commission, offers congratulations to the entire agency. It is as much a speech of congratulations as it is a speech of farewell (this was her last address to employees).

Scoping Document

Event:	Employee meeting
Theme:	Congratulations on a Job Well Done
Place:	Nuclear Regulatory Agency headquarters, Rockville, Maryland
Date:	June 15, 1999
Audience:	Approximately 2,000 NRC employees
Length:	About 6 minutes, 603 words

Speech

At this time last year, the future held some uncertainty, to say the least, and, to some of you, it may have looked downright bleak.

I believe it is to your credit, as members of the NRC staff and NRC management—as well as to the credit of a very hard-working Commission—that today we are an agency once again firmly in control of our own future, clear and confident about the course that lies ahead.

As some of you may be aware, the Senate Appropriations Committee recently approved the NRC full budget proposal, at a time when other agencies are finding their budgets slashed significantly by the same Committee.

Talking Points

Given the speaker's topic, it is a good decision to start off with a disarming, candid statement.

Asserts the reality that the present is good before reviewing the work that led to this point.

So I begin this All Employees Meeting simply by saying, to all of you, "Congratulations on a job well done!"

The topic for the speech: congratulations.

When we were facing budget stringencies and criticism last year, a member of my staff gave me a picture of a sharply meandering road with a caption at the bottom, which read, "a bend in the road is not the end of the road unless you fail to make the turn." We have begun to make the turn. Much remains to be done—but we are turning. So how did we get here?

Starts the review of the hard times. Nice move: quotes an employee, and not one of the commissioners. Asks the question that organizes the remarks to follow.

I would like to spend a few minutes reflecting on the accomplishments of the past year—not only the individual milestones, but also the underlying framework and concepts we have put in place over the past few years which, if understood and implemented consistently, will ensure stability and continued progress as we move forward.

Further gives the audience a sense of what's coming.

At the highest conceptual level are the accomplishments that I would characterize as "achievements of vision."

Lets audience know that they will hear a number of "achievements of vision." It's often good to give the number (3–5) of such topics.

These are the ideals of regulatory excellence; the concept that should be present consistently at all levels of our organization, as well as in all our policies, rules, processes, and individual interactions with our stakeholders.

Indeed, as some of you may recall, regulatory excellence was a key Direction Setting Issue of Strategic Assessment and Rebaselining. Initially we struggled with this concept, but what have we accomplished under this overarching umbrella?

First achievement.

Candor and question for transition to . . . .

The second achievement of vision is a new standard of regulatory effectiveness at the NRC. We have

. . . Second achievement.

become far more introspective and self-critical in examining our own regulations and programs.

Tied directly to NRC regulatory effectiveness is our unapologetic emphasis on performance—what we sometimes refer to as an "outcomes" orientation. We have learned to demand a bottom-line focus on results—both from ourselves and from those we regulate.

Third achievement. The speaker spends about 5 minutes on each achievement (omitted).

The final achievement of vision is our success at anticipating and positioning for change. This element of vision is best characterized by examples, which range from license renewal to our efforts to prepare for electric utility restructuring.

Fourth achievement. The speaker reassures audience with the signal that it's the final one.

I would like to re-emphasize, in closing, the significance of what we have accomplished.

"In closing" is a statement that most audiences love.

I believe that all of you have been aware of and touched by the rapid pace of change across a wide spectrum of NRC functions.

Summing up.

For an agency of this size, with our span of oversight and complexity of functions, to have made this much progress on this many fronts is considered truly remarkable.

Both the short-term and longer term achievements clearly are the result of hard work, innovative thinking, and a commitment to excellence on the part of the Commission, NRC management, and the NRC staff. Whether viewed individually or collectively, these achievements give all of us a glimpse of what we can accomplish, even as they set the stage for continued enhancements in our regulation of nuclear safety and safeguards.

This is but a thumbnail sketch of all we have done.

I thank you for your support and responsiveness to the Commission.

Final expression of gratitude.

10

Elephants *Can* Dance: UPS and Lessons from E-Commerce Alliances

Michael Eskew, United Parcel Service

"It's collaborate or suffocate." That's the main point of this speech. But the subtext is a celebration of the values and achievements of United Parcel Service. Here's another speech that uses the metaphor of an elephant to very good effect. The more a speech uses a concrete metaphor, the more effective it can be. Eskew is vice chairman of United Parcel Service. His remarks were presented to the Conference Board's 2001 Strategic Alliances Conference in New York City on March 28, 2001.

Scoping Document

Event: Conference Board's 2001 Strategic Alliances Conference

Theme: Partnering and Supply Chain Management

Place: New York, New York

Date: March 28, 2001

Audience: Approximately 250 attendees of the Strategic Alliances Conference, mostly CEOs and senior managers

Length: About 15 minutes, 1,453 words

Speech

About ten years ago, author James Belasco wrote a business bestseller called *Teaching the Elephant to Dance.*

It was all about managing a big company to embrace change. I suppose he chose the elephant analogy to illustrate how big, lumbering companies typically lack agility and don't respond quickly to change.

Talking Points

Creates context by referring to well-known work.

I doubt that even Mr. Belasco anticipated the kind of changes that would be jolting companies a decade later.

How the Internet would transform their supply chains from "manual" to electronic . . . and make their business models dependent on a chain of business partners.

With the rise of "c-commerce" . . . or "collaborative commerce" . . . corporate elephants not only have to dance, we have to perform choreographed numbers in perfect rhythm with other elephants.

Ten years ago, the kind of cross-company collaboration and e-commerce alliances we're seeing today would have seemed as strange as a stage full of elephants moving in lock-step.

Let me ask you, what if someone had come up to you ten years ago and suggested that you share your information systems with other companies? Or hand over information about your customers?

Engage audience by asking a question.

You would have thrown him out on his ear.

Now, what if someone had suggested that you outsource your entire supply chain to a third-party logistics provider? You would have thought they were crazy.

Continues line of provocative questions.

But these are precisely the kind of radical steps that companies of all sizes are taking today.

Transition to the new reality and subject of the speech.

Since the early 1990s, the percentage of revenue that the 1,000 largest companies in this country have earned from alliances has more than doubled.

From just 2 percent in 1980, they predict that—by next year—about 35 percent of big-company revenues will flow from alliances.

Ask the strategists from any of these companies, and they'll tell you why they've given up on trying to do everything themselves. It has to do with speed-to-market, instant expertise, global expansion and risk reduction.

Listen to them, and they'll tell you: it's collaborate . . . or suffocate.

But I'll let the other elephants speak for themselves.

I'm here today to talk about the alliance experiences of one particular big, brown 94-year-old, indigenous animal called UPS.

Brings in UPS for the first time.

While I'm not sure I like the elephant description, I have to admit that the size fits . . . .

Supports that statement with details about UPS, omitted here.

If you think about it, a commercial transaction always involves three components: goods, information and funds.

Rule of three. Three components simply introduced and then fleshed out.

All three levels are involved in just about every transaction on the planet. You nearly always have a physical transfer of goods or services that flows from suppliers to customers.

Someone, or some organization, has to make sure raw materials get from supplier to manufacturer . . . that inventory is sent to the right warehouse . . . or that goods go to the right distributors, retailers or end customers.

Component number 1.

The second flow of commerce involves the exchange of information about the goods or services being sold.

Component number 2.

The third component of any transaction involves the exchange of funds. The customer pays the seller. The seller pays the other suppliers. The suppliers pay their lending organizations.

Component number 3.

At UPS, our expanded strategy is to be involved in all three levels of commerce: goods, information and funds. We want to be involved any time, any place in the supply chain where we can add value for our customers. We want to become, in essence, the "operating system" for the 21st Century.

Ambitious, you say?

Short question can be grabbing.

Well, you're absolutely right. Even a company the size of UPS can seem small when chasing a $3 trillion-dollar opportunity.

And let me be perfectly honest. My company is not equipped to exploit this market opportunity. We don't have all the know-how. We're not comfortable with all the risks.

And, since we're being honest, UPS can't say for sure how exactly electronic commerce will transform business models ten years from now.

But we do have a plan to overcome our deficiencies. In the words of James Belasco, we have a way to make the elephant dance.

Tying elephant theme together.

We're going to need help from other companies. In fact, this is going to be an extension of a collaboration strategy we've been pursuing for a few years now.

UPS has been actively seeking out e-commerce alliances since around 1996, when some of our customers came to us and asked for help in creating online, direct-order catalogs.

So we joined together with companies like Harbinger to offer catalog e-commerce software, complete with integrated UPS shipping.

Just as we have in the past, we're going to rely on three different types of e-commerce alliances.

Promises to discuss three types of alliances.

We'll depend on three kinds of partners we describe as Channel Changers, Market Enablers and Trail Blazers.

Promises to talk about three kinds of partners.

Channel Changers are the type of alliances that give you another way to access your customers—that open up new channels to your customer base or to new prospects. These alliances usually involve integrating your own product or service with the products or services of supply-chain partners.

Alliance number 1.

Channel changer alliances are almost always mutually beneficial. It's not all that hard, by the way, to identify potential channel changer partners.

Offers examples of eBay and Oracle (omitted).

In those cases, we rely on the second type of alliance partner—the *Market Enabler.*

Alliance number 2.

A market enabler alliance is the kind that gives you a capability you don't already have—nor necessarily have the expertise to invent yourself.

Offers examples (omitted).

Gaining knowledge is also the objective of a third type of e-commerce alliance—what I call the *Trail Blazer.*

Alliance number 3.

Trail blazer alliances involve investing financially in companies with promising, emerging technologies and services. That was a big impetus behind the launch of our venture capital fund. Through our Strategic Enterprise Fund, we currently invest in 13 companies.

What we learn through these investments could provide a blueprint for the future direction of our company. Or more likely just help us understand where technology is going.

Offers examples (omitted).

Whether the alliance was a channel changer, a market enabler or a trail blazer, we've learned over the years that there are some essential ingredients that determine success.

Repeating three alliance types not only refreshes people's memories but signals transition.

We've learned that it's important to ask yourself four questions about your potential alliance partner . . . and then see if you like the answers.

Transition now to four questions.

Let's go through these four questions.

Announces series of four questions.

Question number one: Do they pass the dinner test? Are your main alliance contacts the kind of people you would invite for dinner in your home? In other words, does your gut tell you that you can trust these people? If not, get away . . . fast.

Question number 1.

Can you trust your partner? If you think you can trust your alliance partners, take it one step further. As Ronald Reagan said of the Soviets: "Trust, but verify."

Quotation.

Get your alliance commitments in detail—and in writing. After all, your trusted contacts might just leave the company, and you're left dealing with people you don't know.

Question number two: Are you keeping your eyes on the prize?

Question number 2.

Question number three: Are you buttering the bread on both sides?

Question number 3.

Question number four: How good is the visibility of your information systems within the alliance? Do all the partners have access to the same systems, the same view of the supply chain? If the platforms are not open, there's no way your supply chain can function in harmony.

Question number 4.

There is no way the elephants can dance.

Back to elephant theme.

Visibility comes from information systems that connect with each other, talk the same language, and share the same data.

UPS had an alliance with a major B2B online marketplace that went dormant for a while when the partner switched to an XML platform.

Example at this point is imperative.

At the time, we couldn't deliver our shipping and tracking functionality in XML. The alliance ceased until we could agree on a mutual platform.

The nearly 200-year-old words of Frances Scott Key . . . "Oh, Say Can You See" . . . are words to live by when it comes to integrating systems with your alliance partners. In fact, answer all four of these questions, and you'll have a better chance of forming a lasting alliance.

Quotation.

Speaking of visibility, I'm reminded of the old parable about the blind men and the elephant.

The elephant parable is a bit overused, but it works here because of the extended elephant metaphor.

One blind man felt the elephant's leg and declared that the creature was like a tree. Another felt the enormous side and said that the elephant is like a wall.

The third, feeling the tail, was positive the elephant was like a rope. Another felt the tusk and thought it was a spear.

Wouldn't it be nice if our alliances were like that elephant—each member performing a separate function but blending seamlessly into a greater whole?

Concluding question.

I'm here to tell you that—with the right kind of alliances—elephants can be nimble.

Hopeful conclusion.

- They can be graceful and coordinated.
- They can be powerful.

Fulfills promise made at beginning of speech.

Elephants, in short, can learn how to dance.

Memorable, graphic closing line.

11 Salesmanship in the New Economy: Calling All Heroes

Wes Hart, Charter Communications

This speech is a rallying cry in a slow economy. It was delivered by Wes Hart, vice president of advertising sales, Charter Communications, at the group's executive summit meeting on May 15, 2001 in Orlando, Florida. It was written to motivate a dispirited sales force to think differently about the bad sales environment and to recast their estimation of themselves from losers to winners.

Scoping Document

Event:	Charter Communications Executive Summit
Theme:	Boosting Morale of Sales Team
Place:	Orlando, Florida
Date:	May 15, 2001
Audience:	Employees and sales team
Length:	About 12 minutes, 1,173 words

Speech

I have to tell you . . . I am so flattered that you guys got out of bed to come hear me talk at 8:00 in the morning—but then, that's what makes you the winners you are—your willingness to take an extra step, make one more call, and walk one more mile—despite whatever obstacles jump into your path.

Those obstacles can be as big as a thunderstorm that brings the airlines to a standstill . . . or as small as a late wake-up call. But here you are.

These are not only the qualities that make you winners. They are, in fact, the qualities of a hero.

Talking Points

The use of "guys" signals a very informal speech.

A very long opening sentence, but it does the trick of introducing the theme of "winners." Much better to use shorter sentences.

Winners and now heroes.

You've probably never put yourself in that category before, have you? Well, if there was ever a time to start thinking heroic thoughts, the time is now.

Today's near-recessive economy has put every single one of us between a rock and a hard place. We are challenged to keep up the remarkable growth of the last 10 years. And yet we are supposed to do it under worse circumstances than ever.

The economy is part of the problem.

Consumer confidence is down . . .

The challenges listed briefly.

Layoffs are rampant . . .

The dot-com boom is over . . .

And we, as sales professionals, are faced with a seemingly impossible assignment . . . in the face of Old Economy slowdowns we are supposed to create New Economy growth.

Introducing the challenge.

Or, to put it another way . . . while our country's economic leaders are getting the kinks worked out of the New Economy, salespeople like you are asked to retain and grow accounts as if nothing at all has changed since this time last year.

I won't kid you . . . times are tough . . . I know it, you know it, the world knows it.

Now what everyone wants to know is what are we going to do about it?

And so, I ask you today . . . What are we going to do about it?

I don't know about you, but my plan is to go home a hero.

This is going to be an inspiration speech.

In the next 20 minutes or so I am going to tell you about some remarkable people who have found themselves in seemingly devastating situations. And yet somehow, deep inside themselves, they found courage and capabilities they didn't know they had. . . .

Laying out the agenda for the speech relaxes the audience. They know what they are in for.

This first story is about a young boy born in Poland during times of poverty and war. This boy was beset with tragedy from his earliest years.

Inspiration by example. Hero number 1.

His father and mother were peasants. His mother suffered from kidney and heart problems.

Her first child, a boy, was born in 1906. Then an infant daughter was born and died.

Her second son—the hero in this story—was born on May 18, 1920, the year Poland declared victory over their Soviet oppressors.

His school friends nicknamed him "Lolek," and he was known for his love of the Polish people, their language and their theater tradition.

Where is all this leading?

He also loved to play soccer. But Lolek's childhood was not destined to be an easy one.

Lolek's mother was not only in bad health, but she also spent hours in bed, suffering from depression. Lolek felt deprived by his mother's illnesses and years later he admitted in an interview that his mother was a sick woman and that she didn't have much time to devote to him.

Continues biography of Lolek.

Lolek himself had two close brushes with death. He was hit once by a streetcar and again by a truck while he was in college. The injuries left him with a noticeable stoop.

There is a Polish saying that "Suffering is crucial for understanding." Our friend Lolek is living proof. His full name is Karol Joseph Woylita, we know him as Pope John Paul II.

Finally puts it together.

The next hero I would like to introduce you to is Erik Weihenmayer. You may have read about Erik in a recent issue of *Sports Illustrated*.

Hero number 2.

Just a few weeks ago, Erik left his home, his wife, and his baby daughter Emma, to start a historic climb of the world's highest mountain. Erik hopes to reach the summit in mid-May, and by the time of his return to Colorado in June, his baby Emma will be much changed. Crawling, certainly. Walking, maybe.

Erik has never actually seen his child, who friends have nicknamed the Gerber Baby.

You see, Erik the mountain climber is blind.

There isn't much about Erik that connects with traditional stereotypes of blind people. In high school, he was Connecticut's second-ranked wrestler in his weight class. He's run marathons. He's made nearly 50 solo skydives . . .

Offers more detail about Erik.

But heroism is not confined to people with disabilities. Take Craig Keilberger of Toronto.

Hero number 3.

When Craig read about the murder of a child who had spoken out against child labor among Pakistan's carpet weavers, he didn't set out to start a global movement.

He just knew something had to be done.

So Craig formed Free the Children, a nonprofit organization dedicated to the elimination of child labor. Craig believes that child exploitation is really about politics, and that if other countries made it clear that child labor is unacceptable, then Pakistan's problem wouldn't exist. Nor would it be happening anywhere else . . .

Offers more detail about Craig.

As if all this weren't enough to make Craig a hero, let me give you one more detail . . .

When Craig started Free the Children, he was only 12 years old.

Saves surprising fact for emphasis.

Wonder how many times Craig was told he was too young to make a difference?

We know he faced significant political and financial hurdles. But he also drew courage and commitment from his passionate concern for abused kids, and—in the process—found success. And made himself a hero.

While our specific hurdles to success are different from those of Lolek, or Erik, or Craig, they are also the same in terms of what they ask of us as human beings. They ask us to stretch our minds beyond the limits of the possible. To embrace the impossible. To become heroes of our own kind. Heroes to our families, our companies and ourselves.

While tough financial times challenge our abilities and try our patience, they also provide us with rare opportunities to take heroic measures and achieve heroic results.

Winston Churchill said, "I know history will be kind to me . . . because I intend to write it."

Quotation. Audiences like to know the source of quotations.

That is exactly the kind of opportunity we have now.

You know, to a large extent, the future success of our enterprise rests on your shoulders. Despite the pundit's gloomy outlook, you are in the right place, at the right time, with the right set of capabilities to create a heroic outcome.

Note the "Rule of Three," which we will encounter in every great speech. Note the repetition: "the right place, the right time, the right set of capabilities." Putting thoughts in groups of three facilitates an appealing rhythm.

In the end, this message is as timeless as everything else you do: the value you add, the relationships you build, the dreams you help make come true.

Rule of three again.

To quote Walt Disney, "It's kinda fun to do the impossible." I'd like to add that doing the impossible is what makes this business fun.

Quotation.

There is no place I would rather be right now than standing before you, looking out at this amazing group of people.

I am proud of each and every one of you—you are my heroes.

Ends with a reference to the word "hero" used in the opening of the speech.

12 Building and Managing a Global Corporation for the New Era

Michael R. Bonsignore, Honeywell

Michael R. Bonsignore is chairman and chief executive officer of Honeywell, Inc. His remarks were presented to the Economic Strategy Institute Global Forum 2000, in Washington, D.C., on May 15, 2000.

Scoping Document

Event: The Economic Strategy Institute Global Forum 2000

Theme: Building and Managing a Global Corporation for the New Era

Place: Washington, D.C.

Date: May 15, 2000

Audience: Approximately 250 Chicago-based chief executives and senior managers

Length: About 9 minutes, 891 words

Speech

We are here tonight at this exciting global forum for one very important reason—because none of us are satisfied with the status quo of this blue marble of a planet we call home.

My task tonight is to address the daunting topic of building and managing a global corporation for the "new era."

But since the temperature of tonight's dinner hinges on the timely delivery of my message . . . I decided to forgo the usual business school micro-lecture on managing global change.

Talking Points

Start with a striking image, e.g. "Blue marble of a planet."

Announces subject of speech right up front.

Audience will be glad that they will be spared a lecture.

Instead, I thought I might take a slightly different approach starting with a very short historical perspective. If I am an internationalist—and I am—it is, in part, because Honeywell has been operating in the international arena for more than 85 years.

Gets corporate plug in early. Remember who you represent.

I spent a number of years in Brussels as president of Honeywell Europe. I've also traveled to nearly all of the 100 countries in which Honeywell does business. My international exposure is invaluable to me in understanding and reacting to the global change around me.

Adds just enough personal detail.

Our recent merger with Allied Signal has created a diverse global enterprise of 120,000 employees doing business around the world with sales of nearly $24 billion last year . . .

Describes merger with Allied Signal.

In the business world, just as in physics, for every action there is a reaction. This evening, however, I'm going to expand that theorem.

In the "physics" of globalization, for every action there is now a . . . chain reaction of consequences— much like this Rubik's cube.

Another strong image.

Each move we make affects another block, another pattern, another side. Likewise, a business decision in one country can affect a worker, a market, a government or a culture a world away.

When CEOs make decisions, we do more than initiate a sequence of actions over time. Rather, we witness an immediate exponential result as these actions affect global economic, political and social relationships.

Turn a Rubik's cube, and you're making a single move but one that also rearranges the pattern of as many as 21 squares. Solving the puzzle requires the ability to see the effect of more than one simple move at a time.

Similarly, the better a company is at anticipating the global effects of its actions, the more successful it's likely to be. One of the great lessons of the 90's is the realization that while the global economy is interconnected, it is not a zero-sum game.

So, as a CEO charged with leading a global corporation, when I make a decision—when I turn Honeywell's cube—it may be in the best interests of my shareowners, but it could upset a government or conflict with a culture on the other side of the globe.

It could ignore new technology, break the rules, and do little to help people. Or just the opposite or a combination—some good and some bad.

Let me give you an example. Both developed and developing nations want clean air. So do environmental groups and business. Some governments and groups would impose unilateral sanctions on emerging nations to achieve clean air. That might help decrease pollution. It might also have a negative effect on a struggling economy.

Every global stakeholder from the smallest government to the largest labor union to the loudest street protestor is part of this chain reaction linked through trade, tradition, and, now, technology.

I also believe, however, that the world's stake-holders are not nearly as far apart as it might seem at times. Listen to these two quotes.

Extends the metaphor. Whenever possible, use a well-known physical artifact to make a complex point.

Transition statement.

Never let audience move too far from the central, unifying image.

When you offer an example, say so.

"Ending child prostitution, slavery, debt bondage, pornography is one of the most urgent demands of our time."

Quotations will be credited, but for now the audience is left wondering.

And the second, "Children must not be subjected to slavery, bondage, prostitution, drug trafficking and extremely hazardous forms of work."

Two quotes come from two so-called "antagonists."

Provocative way to communicate that the sides are closer than we may think.

The first from AFL-CIO President John Sweeney. The second from a joint letter written by The Business Roundtable, the U.S. Chamber of Commerce, and the National Association of Manufacturers, among others.

The truth is—most of us share common concerns—education, open markets, a cleaner world, health care, and poverty.

Our individual facets create individual views of the world's problems; their causes and their solutions.

Back to Rubik's cube image.

So, let me propose three actions that may help us do that—a Brief Manifesto for Global Economic Engagement.

Transition statement as speaker proposes three recommendations. Better to name them first.

First, let us commit to a social compact for global prosperity . . .

Recommendation number 1. Details omitted.

But if business is to play this essential social role, it must do so in the proper environment, which brings me to the second point of this manifesto.

Recommendation number 2. Details omitted.

Albert Einstein is supposed to have given a test when he was teaching at Princeton that confused one of his graduate students. The young man raised his hand and said, "Professor Einstein, these are the

Quotation.

same questions you gave us last year." Einstein smiled and said, "Yes, but the answers are different."

The third challenge in this manifesto is movement toward more open, free-market societies.

Recommendation number 3. Details omitted.

I don't know if the great Albert Einstein could solve our Rubik's cube of a global economy, but I know this much: The answers to creating a better world for all of us are different than those of 30 or 20 or even 10 years ago.

Back to Rubik's cube metaphor.

The moves are ours to make, but we must make them understanding that for every action, there is a chain reaction that will help or hinder the very future of mankind.

Concludes with a call to action.

Freely Connecting the World Through Commerce: A Response to the Seattle Protestors

Jim Kelly, United Parcel Service

Meetings of such bodies as the World Trade Organization (WTO), the World Bank, and the International Money Fund (IMF) have become targets for protestors who are suspicious of the global economy and sometimes dramatize these suspicions. Violence frequently erupts among the demonstrators, as Jim Kelly, chairman and chief executive officer of United Parcel Service, encountered at the WTO forum in Seattle. He decided to address these phenomena by talking about the virtues of both globalization and open dialogue. His remarks were presented to the Town Hall of Los Angeles, February 25, 2000.

Scoping Document

Event:	Town Hall of Los Angeles
Theme:	Globalization and Antiglobalization
Place:	Los Angeles Convention Center, Los Angeles, California
Date:	February 25, 2000
Audience:	Approximately 1,000 attendees of a town hall meeting
Length:	About 14 minutes, 1,335 words

Speech

When I think of Greater Los Angeles I think of Marshall McLuhan's famous phrase, "The Global Village."

Because I can't think of a phrase to describe this community that could be any more precisely *wrong*. You're more what I'd call . . . *the local universe*. Culture, goods, ideas, people, language, politics,

Talking Points

Introduction that combines a comparison with a quotation.

But uses quote to disagree with it.
Defines a new term.

terrific Thai food. If you can't reach it, have it delivered. That's local.

Los Angeles isn't where you live. It's how you live. In fact, this may be the world's first physical prototype of the virtual world.

"The World Wide Web of Los Angeles." Why not?

When you're open to anything and wired to everything, word gets out. Talent is mobile. Knowledge is mobile.

Capital is mobile. No wonder more than 14 million people have made the Basin their home.

That's a universe.

Singapore's minister of trade, George Yeo, puts Los Angeles on the short list, with Shanghai, Singapore, Sydney and Hong Kong, of places capable of sustaining themselves as nation-states. Answer to no one. Attract what you need.

Note use of short sentence fragments.

What all of this means to me as your guest today . . . is simple. It means the Town Hall of Los Angeles is the right place for me to stand up and say a few words from my head and my heart . . . about freely connecting the world, through commerce.

Establishes credentials for what he is about to say.

My perspective as CEO of a company deeply involved in global commerce tells me a connected world would be, on balance, a very good thing, for some reasons I'll mention.

Identifies his perspective.

I was in Seattle last December, at the World Trade Organization meeting. In case you didn't hear what happened at the negotiations inside, I can tell you there wasn't much consensus.

Transition to personal observation.

I guess everyone knows what happened outside in the meantime. Riots. Tear gas. Civil disobedience on the streets of Seattle. And one faction with signs that said, "The WTO kills people. Kill the WTO."

Short, staccato phrases convey the violent drama of the demonstrations.

At first I wondered if that spoke for them all. But in truth it spoke just for those few. Because the scene *outside* was like the scene *inside*. Not much consensus.

Plenty of spirit and passion, though, almost like an anti-nuclear protest. Which befits the target. Listen to this.

"With the possible exception of nuclear weapons, capitalism is the most powerful of human inventions."

Quotation. Identifies the source in the next sentence.

That's the second sentence in Edward Luttwak's new book, *Turbo-Capitalism*.

I agree. That is indeed the duty of responsible business. And I admit it got under my skin for the people on the streets of Seattle to suggest I might believe otherwise.

Here he agrees. Good to note because the audience has been conditioned that the speaker disagrees with quotes.

So I left town a bit troubled. I figured one of two things had happened. One, simply that everything new gets into trouble. Or two, we were watching the eruption of unfocused fear.

Both, probably. *The Economist* recently described the WTO as the new "whipping boy for practically every interest group everywhere." After Seattle, I'm afraid I agree.

. . . But may I suggest we all take a deep breath? Then start a discussion about what economic globalization really portends.

Transition by focusing on breathing. Speaker is effective if he models the behavior he recommends to the audience.

- If it means risking the health of the planet—what are the dangers, and the best plans to avert them?
- If it means changing what we mean by community—what's wrong with that, and what's right?
- If it means putting cultures in peril of extinction—how do we distill what's unique in the world, instead of diluting it out of existence?

Sincere discussion leads to common ground and separates fear from fact. We could use it.

For the sake of discussion, then: Here's where I stand.

Announces his personal convictions.

First—I agree with Luttwak. The virtues of capitalism are in fact unmatched. With wealth comes freedom, and with freedom, justice. This isn't empty rhetoric. It's historical fact. No amount of rioting can do as much to lift the human condition out of suffering poverty as a little dose of economic liberation.

Numbers them, signaling to the audience that it will be a small list.

I will stand and argue with anyone who will listen that economic prosperity is every bit a human right as life, liberty and the pursuit of happiness.

Those who believe that economic prosperity and human rights are mutually exclusive are headed down a slippery slope.

Let me also add that while I'm bothered by some of the *behavior* I saw in Seattle . . . I respect the concern of the protestors. And I respect their opinions. I just think they're wrong . . . assuming I understand them correctly.

Highly nuanced position.

So let me lay out what I believe I heard, and alongside lay out some thoughts of my own.

Starts another list.

First, I sensed an assumption that free global markets are evil.

Point number 1.

Blocking free markets amounts to a breach of freedom.

I found it ironic that . . . and misguided . . . that the unions took such an anti-trade position in Seattle. Trade creates jobs. Union jobs.

At UPS, for example, a job is created for every 30 packages imported to the United States. And it's likely a union job.

First mention of his company.

I also sensed in Seattle a basic misunderstanding of what motivates business.

Point number 2.

Take for instance the protester who explained to reporters that the WTO conspires against consumers—like the Big Three in Detroit conspired with oil companies to suppress a new carburetor that would let cars get 100 miles per gallon.

I'm confused. What car maker wouldn't knock everyone flat to get that carburetor to market?

Very effective to claim confusion instead of going for ridicule.

Let me tell you about a revolution you'll see in your lifetime that will turn practically every rule of business upside down and completely change how you buy.

You know that products today are routinely assembled with parts from all over the world. For everything to come together at the right time and place, each piece has to stick to a precise choreography. In a nutshell, that's supply chain management.

For consumers, the news is even better.

For years, manufacturers have decided what to build, and announced when to line up and buy. That's history. You want that new TV you saw? Log on. Join a web service that uses collective programming. Type in the TV make and model, and presto—you're part of a bargaining group, of 10,000 folks who want the same TV. That's not just a polite little tug on the supply chain. It's a tug-of-war shock that can pull a whole string of manufacturers down into the mud. That's the power the Internet has.

Transition.

That's what business is up against.

But the fact remains: the Internet's unstoppable . . . as unstoppable as globalization.

Does free global trade mean the end of geographic distinction? No. That face expresses a future where distinctions are more valued than ever, and etched in new minds.

Question asked and answered. Note rush to conclusion with repeated use of questions.

Does free trade mean cultural traditions are losing relevance? No. That face expresses how those traditions deepen when the world asks to learn what they mean.

Question and answer.

Does free trade mean the end of individual expression? No. That face expresses the value of things that defy duplication. Globalization isn't so much a goal as it is a path—the inevitable path to a new world. Today, I'm asking for your assistance in helping create this new world.

Question and answer.

Our challenge . . . for each of us in this room . . . is to create a business that is prepared for the new age of commerce. We must also create a business environment that allows our companies to compete fairly in the world marketplace.

Transition away from questions signals conclusion of speech.

I encourage all of us to work together to eradicate obstacles to an integrated international supply chain. Obstacles like outdated policies . . . outdated fears . . . outdated technologies and infrastructures.

Please join me in calling for real lasting change whenever and wherever you see a deterrent to a fair trading system and an efficient supply chain.

. . . Here's my parting question today: Is there hope on the streets of Seattle at all?

Return to theme of Seattle protestors.

I believe there is and so do my colleagues who understand the value of economic connection over division . . . cultural exchange over isolation . . . freedom over protection . . . and trust over suspicion.

For that, the crowds on the streets of Seattle last December might not endorse us, or like us.

Fair enough.

But they can certainly trust us.

So I say let's talk.

Streets of Seattle—what do you say?

In addressing the "Streets of Seattle," the speaker combines two rhetorical devices: personification and synecdoche (letting the part stand for the whole).

PART 2

Articulating the Values of Your Organization

CHAPTER 3

Speeches on Social Responsibility

Speaking about achievements is one of the more agreeable chores of public speaking. People in every community need to celebrate. An effective celebratory speech

- Puts the achievement in context.
- Shares credit with appropriate team members.
- Names names—lists names of deserving individuals.
- Acknowledges the sacrifices, effort, time, or expertise the distinction required.
- Creates a desire in the audience to recreate or emulate the achievement.
- Leads the audience to give thanks and appreciation.
- Lets the audience understand what impact the achievement has on the industry, the organization, and their own careers.

14 | Profiting Through Environmental Balance

Michael Eskew, United Parcel Service

Every organization must confront the tension between pursuing profits and sustaining the environment. In this fairly lengthy speech, Michael Eskew, vice chairman of United Parcel Service, combines a mix of organizational and personal themes to argue that environmental goals are not only good corporate social responsibility but good business, as well. His remarks were presented as the keynote address at the Air & Waste Management Association's 92nd annual meeting in St. Louis.

Scoping Document

Event:	92nd Annual Meeting of the Air & Waste Management Association
Theme:	Environmental Sustainability
Place:	St. Louis, Missouri
Date:	June 21, 1999
Audience:	Approximately 3,000 association members, dignitaries, and media
Length:	About 22 minutes, 2,253 words

Speech

It truly is an honor to be addressing an organization that has done so much to further our understanding of the environment. And you've done so in a way that promotes working cooperation among businesses, governments, and communities.

What I find most impressive is that you've been doing this now for 92 years. You don't stick around 92 years unless you're doing something right. We're very aware of that at UPS.

Talking Points

Indicates the speaker understands the host organization.

Offers compliment and compares achievement to UPS.

In fact, the Air & Waste Management Association and UPS probably have more in common than you might think. For starters, we each were founded way back in 1907 at a time when most environmental philosophies governing business and society were fledgling, at best.

When you can find commonalities, use them.

Needless to say, our respective organizations have grown up with the nation. We've watched trends come and go . . . businesses come and go . . . even communities come and go.

We've also seen our share of rebirth and revitalization, and not just with businesses and communities. We've seen it with managerial thinking and environmental practices.

That last point is what I really want to focus on this morning. I want to explore a new way of thinking about the challenges that confront us as technologists . . . business leaders . . . policy makers . . . and environmentalists. I want to explore a new way of thinking about the concept of balance.

Announces theme of speech.

The topic word: balance.

In preparing for this morning's talk, and the thought of coming back to St. Louis, I felt like a kid again. I grew up about 130 miles directly east of here in a little town along the Wabash River — Vincennes, Indiana.

Starts with personal memories. Note that the speaker ends with same personal themes.

It's a nice town; it's rich in history and agriculture. Vincennes was the place where George Rogers Clark defeated the British in 1779 and freed up the Northwest Territory for American settlement.

About the time UPS and the Air & Waste Management Association were getting started, Vincennes was also known as the pearl capital of the

But make sure to tie the personal memories into the theme of the speech as quickly as possible.

United States. At least that's what the old-timers in town would tell us.

The mussels that lined the river bottom produced pearls that were used commercially for buttons and other accessories. Every once in a while a Wabash River mussel would produce a necklace-quality pearl, fetching as much as $5,000 back in 1907.

But the pearl industry faded long before I ever walked the banks of my hometown river. In essence, the rich soil the Wabash helped produce ultimately choked the river. As agriculture grew, so did runoff from fertilizers and soil. Crops thrived, but the mussels died, and so did the pearl industry.

Like many Midwestern kids, I learned at an early age about the balance of nature and industry, and how fragile that balance can be . . . and the implications it has for people and the land.

Ties theme of balance to personal anecdote.

Today, "balance" might be the most important word in the environmental vocabulary.

About 16 years ago, a bright young filmmaker by the name of Godfrey Reggio released what some folks have called the most remarkable environmental film ever made. It was called *Koyaaniqatsi.* Perhaps some of you have seen it. It won all kinds of awards, even though it had a relatively short life in the theaters.

Speaker elaborates on balance theme in memorable way.

The title was derived from the Hopi Indian word meaning "life out of balance." For 87 minutes, Reggio takes you through a cinematic journey that almost defies description. There are no words and no plot. It's just extraordinary images of the world's natural environment, then human encroachment,

and technology run amok, and then finally, chaos.
Life and nature wind up completely out of balance.

It's a startling experience, albeit perhaps a little
heavy handed. I, for one disagree that technology is
ruining the environmental balance. Just the opposite
is the case. I think technology will probably help
save it. And over the next several minutes, you're
going to hear plenty of examples of technology
advances that are cleaning up corporate America
and the environment.

*Promises audience what it will
see and hear.*

We need change that recognizes that the long-term
fate of the global environment and the global economy are mutually dependent, not mutually exclusive.

Now, let me start by saying I'm not an environmental
expert. And I certainly don't have a blueprint to save
the earth and our businesses with the wave of a
wand. But I can share with you some ideas to get us
all thinking more about how technology, business,
government, and society can restore balance and create meaningful change as the environmental movement enters the 21st century.

*Speaker disarms audience by
acknowledging his lack of credentials as an expert and reassures them by expressing
confidence in what they will
learn.*

In our view at UPS, there are at least three key areas
we need to address to create the kind of balance that
promotes lasting environmental protection and economic opportunities for future generations. They're
simple concepts, really. It starts with education . . .
seeking the truth. It requires leadership . . . the willingness and courage to take action. And it requires
an understanding of the environmental supply chain,
and the financial impact of working greener and
smarter.

*Promises to talk about three
areas.*

*Organizes balance of speech in
three points. Announces them
here and then fills out each
point with details.*

Let's start with the first area, educating and inform-
ing. You might call it "breaking down the myths,"

Point number 1: Education.

"getting the facts straight," or even, "getting politics out of the process."

Like a lot of you folks out there, I'm an engineer and a business person. I'm trained to look at problems and then find solutions. Finding solutions that work are impossible without first clearly identifying the problems. That's a huge challenge today in the environmental movement.

On the one hand, the doomsayers will tell you the environmental apocalypse is just around the corner. On the other hand, the negligent polluters will tell you it's all a bunch of hullabaloo. That leaves a very wide gap to find the truth. We need to narrow that gap. No one's telling us that louder than our customers.

A recent study commissioned by the National Environmental Education and Training Foundation found that Americans are misinformed and "grossly confused" about environmental issues. According to the study, the average American can correctly answer fewer than 25 percent of questions found on a basic environmental literacy test. That statistic bodes poorest for companies.

I don't typically quote Mark Twain because so many speakers do. But since we're here in his home state, let me try this one on you. Twain said that a rumor can race around the world while the truth is just putting its shoes on.

Quotation.

We're kind of at that stage with environmental myths, aren't we? Some, for example, would have us believe that the air quality in California today is the worst in history. Some would have us believe that we're cutting more trees than we're planting, or that we're killing off all the white-tailed deer.

But there's plenty of empirical evidence to suggest
that California's air is the cleanest in recorded history. There's plenty of evidence to suggest that forest
growth across the U.S. has exceeded harvest since the
1940s, and that we have more forests today than we
had 70 years ago. And there's evidence that we have
more deer and wild turkeys than during the time of
Miles Standish and the first Thanksgiving at
Plymouth Rock.

Startling statistics.

The disparities between the myths and the realities
should frighten us almost as much as some of the
realities themselves. They make it extremely hard,
and sometimes impossible, for folks like us to devise
and implement solutions to real problems.

Education, of course, is the key to overcoming this
problem. The more we know, the more we're
engaged to seek the truth. UPS works with a host of
environmental education groups, not only to learn
more about the issues, but also to seek their counsel
in solving some of the challenges that confront our
business.

The marketplace is demanding corporate leadership.
For those of us in business, this adds another dimen-
sion to the idea of being customer-driven, and cus-
tomer-responsive.

*Point number 2: Leadership
should be identified more
explicitly.*

A report on environmental performance and share-
holder value put together by the World Banking
Consortium reinforces this point. It states,
"Environmental issues can drive financial performance through traditional elements of financial evalua-
tions, such as robust and forward-looking strategies,
operational fitness of the company, product quality
and corporate reputation."

At UPS, we've certainly seen the effect on corporate reputation. For the past 16 years, we've been selected by *Fortune* magazine as the most admired company in the transportation industry. One of the eight criteria used in the *Fortune* survey of business executives is a company's attention to social and environmental responsibility.

Take time to play up your company.

For many companies, environmental leadership is producing head-turning financial and competitive benefits. For example, concern about recycling aluminum prompted Anheuser-Busch, right here in St. Louis, to develop a can that's 33 percent lighter. Integrating the manufacturing process into a recycling program is saving the company about $200 million a year.

Good to play up local company.

Success stories such as these abound, but so do tales from the crypt from companies that have disregarded the power of environmental consumerism. There's the story of the huge paper company that lost 5 percent of its sales overnight after an article was published citing its lackluster reforestation and waste reduction efforts.

And there's the cotton producer that lost a multimillion-dollar contract because of its agricultural practices. And there's the international airline that lost a major corporate account because its loud jets were distracting workers at an office park.

UPS recently secured a $3 million contract with Interface. Probably the biggest reason we were awarded that contract was because of the way we were maximizing our transportation efficiencies, which corresponded to greater environmental efficiencies.

Many of these same factors helped close a similar $1.5 million deal with Patagonia. And we realize this is just the tip of the iceberg. There are plenty more customers who seek efficient transportation as an extension of their environmental process improvement.

At UPS, we look at environmental process improvement much like we look at a physical supply chain. In boardrooms around the country, there's a growing awareness that the physical supply chain has become one of the last frontiers for businesses to drive efficiencies and gain competitive advantages. That brings me to the third point in our balance formula, the power of the environmental supply chain.

Point number 3 should be identified more explicitly.

Instead of moving goods, information, and money up and down the supply chain, you're developing environmental efficiencies for yourself and the next link in the chain. A lot of the work you folks are doing in driving eco-efficiencies in your companies and organizations is bearing fruit. Energy efficiency, water conservation, waste minimization, process re-engineering, and environmental design are no longer thought of as fringe elements. They're now part of the mainstream processes in corporate America.

In our business, operating efficiency is an incredible competitive advantage, and it's good for the environment.

Sustainable development, as we now recognize, is dependent on an integrated chain of events . . . from the source, all the way to the end consumer. I'll take my own industry as an example.

As a package delivery company that operates more than 150,000 vehicles and a fleet of more than 500

Provides more context for UPS.

airplanes, we have a great responsibility to lessen our imprint on the environments of the 200 countries we serve every day. We're doing our part. But there's plenty more to be done . . . by us and by other partners in our environmental supply chain.

All of this requires a lot of cross-industry partnerships. They are partnerships based on trust, knowledge of the issues, and real leadership. You might have inferred from my previous statement that I was picking on the oil and auto industries. Let me assure you, I wasn't.

You know, when I was a kid, coming to St. Louis was the highlight of our summers. I made my first trip across the flat farmlands of southern Illinois (the land between the rivers) when I was 8 or 9. Of course, my two brothers and I came to see the Cardinals play baseball. But for that first trip, my mom tried to mix in some diversity and culture, so she scheduled a day at the ballpark, and a day at the zoo.

Back to personal theme signals transition.

On our way home from that first trip, mom asked, "What did you boys think of the zoo?" And I answered, "Mom, I'd rather watch two ballgames." Well, as kids, we never did go back to the zoo.

But more recently in the baseball film, *Field of Dreams*, the James Earl Jones character said to the Kevin Costner character, *"The only constant is baseball."*

I had always agreed with that, and that felt so familiar. Now, thanks to UPS, I've called ten places home since I left Vincennes, and in each of those places I've found myself rooting for "the home team" — even American League teams.

But with that experience, I've come to realize that James Earl Jones was wrong and my mom, of course, was right. And now I finally get it, *"The only constant is the zoo."*

As a matter of fact, later this summer, UPS will be moving a pair of Panda bears from Beijing to Atlanta as part of an educational and research initiative being developed by Dr. Terry Maple of Zoo Atlanta. Dr. Maple is attempting to break down some of the myths behind Panda behavior, with the ultimate goal of helping to save an endangered species.

Closes with memorable image of UPS tied to the speaker's heartfelt anecdotes. Excellent conclusion.

15 The Armor of Integrity

General Charles C. Krulak, USMC (Ret.)

General Krulak, USMC (ret.), is former Commandant of the Marine Corp and served as senior vice chairman of MBNA America. This is not a fluff speech. It makes demands on an audience, perhaps not unsurprising given the speaker's military experience. It's important to remember that even in the military audiences cannot be commanded to listen. Fortunately, in this case, General Krulack has a lot to say and backs it up with evidence and appeals to even higher authority.

Scoping Document

Event:	The Joint Services Conference on Professional Ethics
Theme:	Professional Ethics
Place:	Springfield, Virginia
Date:	January 27, 2000
Audience:	Approximately 1,000 business leaders and media
Length:	About 10 minutes, 1,055 words

Speech

We study and we discuss ethical principles because it serves to strengthen and validate our own inner value system.

It gives direction to what I call our moral compass. It is the understanding of ethics that becomes the foundation upon which we can deliberately commit to inviolate principles.

It becomes the basis of what we are . . . of what we include in our character. Based on it, we commit to doing what is right. We expect such commitment from our leaders. But most importantly, we must demand it of ourselves.

Talking Points

Starts by defining the themes of the remarks.

Sound morals and ethical behavior cannot be established or created in a day . . . a semester . . . or a
year. They must be institutionalized within our character over time . . . they must become a way of life.
They go beyond our individual services and beyond
our ranks or positions; they cut to the heart and to
the soul of who we are and what we are and what we
must be . . . men and women of character. They arm
us for the challenges to come and they impart to us a
sense of wholeness. They unite us in the calling we
now know as the profession of arms.

Of all the moral and ethical guideposts that we have
been brought up to recognize, the one that, for me,
stands above the rest . . . the one that I have kept in
the forefront of my mind . . . is integrity. It is my ethical and personal touchstone.

Integrity as we know it today, stands for soundness of
moral principle and character—uprightness—honesty. Yet there is more. Integrity is also an ideal . . . a
goal to strive for . . . and for a man or woman to
"walk in their integrity" is to require constant discipline and usage.

Defines integrity *as the focus of the speech.*

The word *integrity* itself is a martial word that comes
to us from an ancient Roman Army tradition.

A little military history lesson.

During the time of the 12 Caesars, the Roman Army
would conduct morning inspections. As the inspecting Centurion would come in front of each
Legionnaire, the soldier would strike with his right fist
the armor breastplate that covered his heart. The
armor had to be strongest there in order to protect the
heart from the sword thrusts and from arrow strikes.

As the soldier struck his armor, he would shout
"*integritas*," which in Latin means material whole-

ness, completeness, and entirety. The inspecting Centurion would listen closely for this affirmation and also for the ring that well-kept armor would give off. Satisfied that the armor was sound and that the soldier beneath it was protected, he would then move on to the next man.

At about the same time, the Praetorians or imperial bodyguard were ascending into power and influence. Drawn from the best "politically correct" soldiers of the legions, they received the finest equipment and armor. They no longer had to shout "*integritas*" to signify that their armor was sound. Instead, as they struck their breastplate, they would shout "Hail Caesar," to signify that their heart belonged to the imperial personage—not to their unit—not to an institution—not to a code of ideals. They armored themselves to serve the cause of a single man.

A century passed and the rift between the legion and the imperial bodyguard and its excesses grew larger. To signify the difference between the two organizations, the legionnaire, upon striking his armor would no longer shout "*integritas*," but instead would shout "*integer*."

Integer means undiminished—complete—perfect. It not only indicated that the armor was sound, it also indicated that the soldier wearing the armor was sound of character. He was complete in his integrity . . . his heart was in the right place . . . his standards and morals were high.

He was not associated with the immoral conduct that was rapidly becoming the signature of the Praetorian Guards.

The armor of integrity continued to serve the legion well. For over four centuries they held the line against the marauding Goths and vandals but by 383 AD, the social decline that infected the republic and the Praetorian Guard had its effects upon the legion. As a 4th century Roman general wrote, "when, because of negligence and laziness, parade ground drills were abandoned, the customary armor began to feel heavy since the soldiers rarely, if ever, wore it.

Transition to the modern concept of integrity.

Integrity . . . it is a combination of the words, *integritas* and *integer*. It refers to the putting on of armor, of building completeness . . . wholeness . . . wholeness in character. How appropriate that the word integrity is a derivative of two words describing the character of a member of the profession of arms.

Now comes the time to make the point.

The military has a tradition of producing great leaders that possess the highest ethical standards and integrity. It produces men and women of character . . . character that allows them to deal ethically with the challenges of today and to make conscious decisions about how they will approach tomorrow.

However, as I mentioned earlier, this is not done instantly. It requires that integrity becomes a way of life . . . it must be woven into the very fabric of our soul. Just as was true in the days of imperial Rome, you either walk in your integrity daily, or you take off the armor of the *Integer* and leave your heart and soul exposed . . . open to attack.

My challenge to you is simple but often very difficult . . . wear your armor of integrity . . . take full measure of its weight . . . find comfort in its protection . . . do not become lax. And always,

Here's the inevitable challenge to the audience.

always, remember that no one can take your
integrity from you . . . you and only you can
give it away!

The biblical book of practical ethics—better known
as the Book of Proverbs—sums it up very nicely:
"The integrity of the upright shall guide them: But
the perverseness of transgressors shall destroy them."

*Ends with a quotation from the
Bible, a fitting conclusion to a
speech on ethics and integrity.*

16 | Unleashing the Power of the Human Mind and Spirit

Earnest W. Deavenport Jr., Eastman Chemical Company

These are the remarks Earnest W. Deavenport, Jr., former chairman and CEO of Eastman Chemical Company, gave when presented with the 1996 Kavaler Award, the chemical industry's highest recognition for executive achievement. In accepting the award, Deavenport challenged industry executives to share success with employees.

Scoping Document

Event:	Chemical Industry Award Dinner
Theme:	Kavaler Award presentation
Place:	Washington, D.C.
Date:	November 14, 1996
Audience:	Chemical industry executives, guests, media
Length:	About 13 minutes, 1,370 words

Speech

It is, indeed, a great honor to receive this year's Kavaler Award. When I told my wife, Mary Ann, about it, she said, "What exactly does this award do?" And I said, "Well, it doesn't *do* anything." And she said, "Then they are giving it to the right person!"

Seriously, it *is* a great honor to be recognized by the petrochemical community and to be included in the company of other Kavaler winners like Bob Kennedy and Jon Huntsman and many, many others who consistently create value for their companies, and by doing so, provide opportunities for their customers to create value, as well.

But each of us has our own distinct method of creating value.

Talking Points

A self-deprecating joke in which the honoree pokes fun at his own qualifications is a tried and true way to set the tone.

Always a good idea to state the purpose of the gathering. Honoring former honorees adds a touch of class.

It's like the story of the woman who didn't have much faith in her husband's ability to make a lot of money, so she bought a lottery ticket every week.

One day she called her husband and said, "Honey, start packing! I hit the jackpot!" And he said, "That's great! But wait . . . should I pack summer clothes for a cruise or winter gear for skiing? And she said, "I don't care what you pack, just be out of the house by morning!"

This joke is a touch edgy. The risk with edgy material is that in the wrong hands it comes off as mean.

In a real sense, a lot of people believe that corporate America creates value that way.

You can turn on the evening news . . . or open any major newspaper to the business page . . . or pick up a business magazine and you'll see stories about layoffs, downsizing, outsourcing, and billion-dollar mergers. And more often than not, these stories describe employees as victims thrown out with no place to go.

That's the rhetoric. But what's the reality?

Asks a question. Introduces topic of speech.

And that's what I want to talk about this evening. I want to talk about the reality of a growing anxiety among millions of American workers who feel they are being disenfranchised by capitalism, and what *we*, as *champions* of capitalism, must do to turn the tide of discontent.

And it's time we started closing the gap between the rhetoric and the reality. Because if this feeling of being short-changed by the success of corporate America continues to grow, the discontented will turn to government for relief. And the last thing our free-market system needs is more government.

The volume has already been turned up on the rhetoric. Stories like those that ran in the *New York Times* this past summer and articles in *Newsweek* and *BusinessWeek* about "Corporate Killers" and "Workers Taking It on the Chin" perpetuate the image of workers as an "anxious class," as the Secretary of Labor Robert Reich likes to describe them.

Rhetoric says that economic change is beating down the American worker. But reality says that economic change is lifting us up! Reality says that our drive to compete has created *twice* as many jobs as any other advanced economy . . . that inflation is the *lowest* in 20 years . . . and that total employee compensation is *up* nearly 15 percent since 1980.

The Federal Reserve tells us that the dynamics of our capitalist system creates a net two million jobs per year, and that nearly one job in six is a "new" job in any given year. Any economy that can remake itself every six years is truly an engine of opportunity.

And while we have done a great job of capitalizing on these opportunities to create value for our shareowners, we could do a better job of communicating that capitalism is more than just a system for creating corporate profits.

Acknowledges where company can do better.

We can close the gap by getting the message out that capitalism is the best system in the world for maximizing the value of technology, for maximizing the value of knowledge, and for maximizing the value of the human mind and spirit.

Look at what capitalism and our free market system has done to make technology available to the average American.

Composite plastics designed for the space program are now used to make mountain bikes and sail boats. Time-release medicines, once the marvel of medical science, are now commonplace. Microwave technology, once a military secret, is now a common kitchen appliance.

Advanced technology like cellular telephones, soft contact lenses, over-the-counter drugs, and compact disks are all available for less than a half-day's pay for the average American worker.

No other system in the world has this ability to make technology more accessible or more affordable than does capitalism.

Now, what about maximizing the value of knowledge? Capitalism thrives on the quest for knowledge. Not for the sake of just knowing, but for the sake of applying knowledge toward bettering one's lot in life.

Another question moves the speech along.

More people are finishing high school, more people are finishing college, and more people are training to upgrade their job skills today than at any time in the past 20 years. Why? Because in our capitalist system, knowledge pays off.

When it comes to maximizing the value of the human mind and spirit, no other economic system even comes close.

Capitalism is the best system on earth for unleashing the power of the human mind and spirit because it's incentive-based. It rewards those who take risks.

Malcolm Forbes once said that it's not taking and consuming, but giving, risking, and creating that characterizes capitalism. And it's the giving, the risk-

Reference. Malcolm Forbes

ing, and the creating that characterize the human mind and spirit.

We are maximizing the value of their ideas and their brain power with incentive pay plans that give all employees an opportunity to create real wealth and to share in the success of their company. Eastman employees act like owners and have the power to make decisions. And I have every reason to believe that Eastman men and women will made the *right* decisions based on their incentives to maximize value. That's what capitalism does best.

Now . . . what more can you and I do to close the gap between the rhetoric and the reality.

We can do three things. As Forbes said . . . We can give. We can risk. And we can create.

Repeats three themes.

We can give our experience, our judgment, and our insights to a broader range of social issues that concern our fellow employees other than just wages and benefits. We have a responsibility to actively engage in national debates and to be a loyal advocate for our employees on such issues as crime, health care, and drugs. The biggest social issue facing the American worker today is not unemployment, but unemployability.

First theme details.

Secondly, we can risk . . . We can risk a chance on a higher rate of economic growth. The root cause of much of the workplace anxiety and the growing discontent with our economic system is that expectations are not being met. And it's because our national economy is growing at a timid 2.5 percent a year.

Second theme details.

And third, we can create. We can create a new socio-economic contract with our employees that

Third theme details.

provides a greater share in the success of Corporate America. If employees have a real stake in the capitalist system, if they share equally in the rewards and the risks, then they will become more innovative, more productive, and more focused on creating real value.

To me, capitalism is the world's best for making the best even better. It maximizes the value of technology. It maximizes the value of knowledge. And it maximizes the value of the human mind and spirit.

And if we, as leaders in one of the most important industries in America, will give of ourselves to issues beyond the bottom line, if we will take a risk on higher growth, and if we create a new socio-economic contract with our employees, we will have gone far in reducing the anxiety that jeopardizes the role that capitalism will play in America's future.

Summary of themes cited.

In closing, let me again thank the petrochemical community for selecting me for this prestigious award.

Transition to closing.

My special thanks to all the men and women of Eastman Chemical Company and to my family, who are the real winners of this award tonight.

Shares the award with his colleagues.

When I think of the contribution this industry has made to the quality of life for hundreds of millions of people, I am gratified and reinforced. When I think of the countless millions whose standard of living will be enhanced in the coming decades, I stand in awe.

Final summary using two parallel statements, each starting with the same word and ending with a flourish.

17 The Meaning of Human Rights

Richard Newton, British Petroleum

Remarks by former British Petroleum executive Richard Newton at an Amnesty International Event in Birmingham, England, on November 1, 1997. After a 32-year career at BP, Newton is currently Senior Associate, University of Cambridge Program for Industry.

Scoping Document

Event:	Amnesty International Conference
Theme:	Human rights
Place:	Birmingham, England
Date:	November 1, 1997
Audience:	Approximately 1,000 business leaders, human rights activists, dignitaries, and media
Length:	About 9 minutes, 910 words

Speech

At the international Vienna Conference on human rights in 1993, Boutros Boutros-Ghali reminded us that "equality of opportunity for development is a prerogative both of nations and of individuals who make up nations . . . the right to development is a human right."

Which is a key role for Business, and we aim to do that well, in a socially and environmentally responsible manner.

But some NGOs and others expect more than that . . . and I will come back to this in a moment.

I want to speak this morning about four major aspects of this issue

Talking Points

Opens with a quotation from a credible source, in this case the former Secretary General of the United Nations.

Transition to the interests of business leaders.

NGO is a nongovernmental organization, such as Amnesty International.

Good to announce the speaker's plan.

107

1. The power of companies to influence governments
2. What we are doing in BP
3. The meaning of human rights
4. And the importance of partnerships and working together.

Lists them.

Firstly . . . the power of companies to influence governments. I am going to quote from a speech made in New York by our Group Chief Executive, John Browne:

And then takes them up one at a time.

"I think it was Bertrand Russell who said that from any particular perspective power always seems to be elsewhere.

Always prudent to quote your boss, even if the boss is quoting someone else!

"Certainly from inside the company it doesn't feel as if we have great power. Companies work within the constraint of a competitive market and open global financial markets have intensified that competition. Natural resource companies are even more constrained than most. We can only explore for oil in the areas where geology has left us something to find.

"I don't think there is any place in the world where we actually own the oil we produce. We work through leases and licenses. If anyone thinks that power in such relationships lies exclusively with the oil companies they should come and see how things work in Venezuela, Azerbaijan, or Alaska. There and elsewhere we can only work successfully if we can persuade the local community that our business brings mutual advantage.

"To say that companies have no power would be as much of a caricature as saying that they are all powerful. If people think you have power—then, to some degree at least, you do. Beyond the question of

This is a long passage to quote from another speech. It might have been better to put all this in the speaker's own voice.

perceptions we undoubtedly have the ability to take independent decisions which affect others—decisions on investments that provide jobs and revenue and, in turn, can affect the fortunes of communities and government, and decisions on how we work which can affect the societies of which we are part."

So we have the power to do some things but not as much as some people think—this is why partnerships are important.

Speaker resumes his own text.

But we see the concern and we are addressing that concern by being explicit about our Policies in a range of areas from ethics to the environment, from employees to community relationships.

Second issue. Might be better for the speaker to be more explicit about the transition.

Our views on human rights are embodied in these Policies.

These are not new Policies but in an organization as diverse as ours we realize we need to be clearer about these Policies and so we are collating them together in one explicit document.

We see this as part of our corporate governance and assurance processes.

We have also established a management structure supporting the Board and our people in their day-to-day dealings with difficult issues.

I want now to talk about the meaning of human rights.

Third issue.

The phrase 'human rights' is often used in terms of one part only of the total picture. It is a crucial part. Nothing should be taken to diminish the focus on the specific civil liberties which are denied to people in so many parts of the world—freedom of speech, freedom of worship, freedom from torture and so on.

But human rights is not a single issue or group of single issues, it is about the development of society as a whole. BP is aware that our environmental and social impact, how we treat our employees, how we deal with others, how we maintain financial integrity, are all part of securing rights for people.

My fourth issue was Partnerships. I want to talk about working together to address human rights issues.

Fourth issue.

And this is self-interest: Ours is both a short- and long-term business. We thrive when societies, consumers, employees, partners, thrive. Safe, stable, secure societies are in our commercial favor.

Words are fine, but we know we must demonstrate that we are behaving in this way by our track record. By being open, by consulting widely, with NGOs, communities, employees, and others, and by reporting our performance. And, we need to develop the means of verification to underpin our own assurance.

Calls for commitment to action.

But even given our Policies and our assurance processes, we of course face difficult decisions on the ground, and public scrutiny.

But first, I want to say that this is an area riddled with difficult judgments and paradoxes. There are virtually no clear-cut issues. Progress therefore will depend heavily on leadership, balanced judgments, and tolerance, and working together.

Gets into cases and discusses the case in Algeria (omitted).

We also mustn't forget that in any country where human rights activists are subject to danger, BP staff can be subject to the same dangers.

I am offering no solutions here, just being open about the issue:

Makes a list.

- How do we defend our operations?
- How do we ensure communities benefit?
- How do we promote human rights when we have little contact with the government and without putting our staff at risk?

Each case is different. Each case is a judgment.

Humble statement as the speech winds down. Transition to end.

In the end, we believe that business is a force for human rights, not against it.

We are very much part of the solution, not the problem.

Conclusion would be better if it were reworded to end with the word solution: *"We want the world to see us not as the problem, but as part of the solution."*

CHAPTER 4

Speeches on Corporate Ethics

Given the meltdown in corporate credibility in the wake of Enron, Worldcom, Tyco, Adelphia, and scores of other scandals, one of the main jobs of leaders at every level of the organization is to regain the trust of the stakeholders. That means speaking the truth, acknowledging past excesses, and making a commitment to transparency. The following speeches all address past abuses in a candid, no-nonsense manner, and in various ways describe how the situation has changed.

18 The Value of Candor

John Bogle, Vanguard

> *In 1990, Vanguard had one of its worst years. Chairman John Bogle took the opportunity to address the employees about the need to confront bad news directly and with candor. Bogle has been called the conscience of the mutual fund industry.*

Scoping Document

Event:	Employee meeting
Theme:	The Value of Candor
Place:	Vanguard headquarters, Valley Forge, Pennsylvania
Date:	December 14, 1990
Audience:	Approximately 2,000 Vanguard employees
Length:	About 2 minutes, 281 words

Speech

One of the most important values is candor—tell the whole truth and nothing but the truth, with no strings attached, and let the chips fall where they may.

Sometimes it feels pretty good.

A year ago, in our annual reports, we told our clients not to expect in the 1990s a repeat of the Gold Decade of the 1980s in which the returns on financial assets were the highest in history.

And as soon as 1990 began, we had sharp declines in the stock and bond markets, followed during the summer by even sharper declines as the Persian Gulf Crisis brought the world to the brink of war.

Talking Points

As direct a statement of candor as is possible.

Disclosure up front.

Shareholders who followed our advice—hold a mix of stocks, bonds, and cash reserves that meets your own goals and risk tolerance, and then stay the course—easily weathered the storm, perhaps bloodied, but nonetheless unbowed.

Sometimes it hurts.

Admit the pain.

Early in 1989, we warned Windsor Fund shareholders to beware of a possible bad year for the fund, noting that no investment account—whoever its manager, whatever its objective—outperforms the stock market consistently, year after year. This warning was borne out not only in 1989 but in 1990, when the fund's stunning decline caused me to begin my letter in the just published annual report with the words, "this is my 21st chairman's letter to you . . . by all odds it is the most difficult one I have ever had to write."

Acknowledge bad times without defensiveness or excuses.

Example of warning.

Just say it straight.

You just don't find these kinds of words or thoughts in the pallid reports of our competitors. But easy or hard, right or wrong, this candor is a simple manifestation of our respect for the intelligence of our clients.

A little dig against his competitors, but Bogle is right.

Simple conclusion of why he believes in candor.

19 Rebuilding Trust Begins with Us

Douglas Daft, Coca-Cola

Douglas Daft is chairman and CEO of The Coca-Cola Company. He joined the company in 1969 as planning officer in the Sydney, Australia office. He was elected president and chief operating officer of The Coca-Cola Company in December 1999. He delivered these remarks to a group of students as part of the Morehouse College Coca-Cola Lecture Series on October 8, 2002.

Scoping Document

Event:	Morehouse College Coca-Cola Lecture Series
Theme:	Rebuilding Trust Begins with Us
Place:	Morehouse College, Atlanta, Georgia
Date:	October 8, 2002
Audience:	Approximately 200 students, faculty, administrators
Length:	About 11 minutes, 1,064 words

Speech

I welcome the opportunity to speak on the issue of corporate responsibility because it is an issue of such vital importance to everyone.

It has become the driving story in the media almost every hour. For all of us, it is one of the most important business issues we will face because it will help define my generation's business legacy to you. And for you, learning now will prepare you to avoid the mistakes of the prior generation.

Simply put: we are living squarely in the middle of a "crisis of trust."

Talking Points

Announces theme of speech up front.

Puts the issue in context. Note contrast of "for all of us" and "for you."

Restates theme and urgency.

The philosopher George Santayana's well-known saying "those who do not remember the past are condemned to repeat it" seems pertinent.

Quotation.

This is a subject worthy of serious comment by academics, thinkers, politicians and spiritual leaders as well as countless others. But I'm a businessman. In fact, I am a CEO—the least honored species these days, one might gather. But I want to take the opportunity to talk about trust and corporate governance by drawing on illustrations from what I know best—and that's my experience at The Coca-Cola Company.

Acknowledges low esteem held by CEOs.

Speaks from experience.

Fundamentally, The Coca-Cola Company is built on a deep and abiding relationship of trust between it and all its constituents: bottlers . . . customers . . . consumers . . . shareowners . . . employees . . . suppliers . . . and the very communities of which successful companies are an integral part. That trust must be nurtured and maintained on a daily basis.

Brings in Coca-Cola.

To be candid, every company from time to time makes mistakes—including The Coca-Cola Company. When we do, we face them and fix them, as we did with the discrimination lawsuit and our renewed and strengthened commitment to diversity.

Admits mistakes and gives an example. Very bold.

And the fact that our audiences are dismayed—even shocked—by the fact that we may have stumbled speaks volumes about the high esteem in which we are held and the strong bond of trust we already had. Indeed, trust is quickly preserved because our constituents see how we fix and do not hide problems. I wouldn't have it any other way.

How do we build that sort of trust? For all of our audiences, it's based on knowing what you stand for . . . and then saying what you'll do and doing what you say.

Asks question and answers it.

Plato said "Good people do not need laws to tell them to act responsibly, while bad people will find a way around the laws." To me, that gets at the heart of knowing what you stand for.

Quotes another philosopher.

It's pretty unambiguous: It's doing what is right.

Simple statement.

If you want the Cliff Notes version of what that means in business life, you can find it in any of the fundamental texts of the world's religions—whether the Bible, Koran, Torah or others.

Because, I assure you of this . . . if you take seriously your ethical and moral grounding, one that forbids you to steal or covet, and encourages you to do right by others, then all the rest will come naturally.

After 120 years of building the world's number one brand, we know that compromising on values undermines a company's ability to create value . . .

Talks about how the value of telling the truth plays out at Coca-Cola (omitted).

That's why we remain so engaged in communities, helping those in need and creating jobs through significant investment.

Rapid series of statements with common leads "That's why. . . ."

That's why we strive for transparency in our financial reporting, as evidenced by our decision earlier this summer, to take a stand and report employee stock options as an expense.

That's why we aim to create a working environment in which the best ideas and diverse perspectives are embraced, not simply tolerated.

That's why we work hard to protect the environment for the benefit of current and future generations.

Ultimately, I see that as the only way to build the trust that is at the heart of a successful business over the long-term.

In this current environment, have the rules changed, as some have suggested?

Another question indicates transition.

I don't believe they have. And I hope this discussion does not strike you as a particularly radical set of ideas.

Yes, the degree of scrutiny has changed. And skepticism is at an unprecedented level. Certainly, the questions are now being asked with more urgency, and, at the moment, people are no longer willing to accept half-answers, spin or marketing-speak.

Acknowledges skepticism.

You see, the challenge . . . it's still the same. People want proof of responsible behavior. They want results. They want to trust their business leaders. And they are more sophisticated than ever before in understanding what companies are doing.

Names the challenge.

And business people must respond—defining ourselves in a way that is true to our values; understanding what is expected of us; and then keeping our promises—again and again and again.

In the future, each of you will be confronted with specific situations that seem to make this difficult.

Turns the challenge back to the audience.

And know that "I was only doing my duty" or "just following orders" is no longer acceptable. Your duty is to do what is right and never be blind to what is wrong.

Responsible leadership is as simple, and as difficult, as that. It requires business leaders to listen to their ethical and moral voice within.

Parents at home and other role models in schools, universities, government and business must play a role in nurturing that voice, in turning up the volume.

Educational institutions in particular must help students explore how challenges can play out in real-life business situations . . . and help teach students how to separate the wheat from the chaff when confronted by a potential dilemma.

They must educate students about the recourses available, so that you can cry out "stop" when necessary, and make the right decision in the face of sometimes powerful pressure.

At the end of the day, you are the next generation of leaders—in business, in academia and government. How will you learn the lessons of today? How will you build trust among your constituents? How will you avoid the painful experiences of those we are reading about in the newspaper?

Transitions with a series of rhetorical questions. The audience doesn't expect the speaker to answer these questions.

One day you will have the opportunity to put your answers into action. And whether you carry us forward or simply repeat the mistakes of today will depend on how effectively you listen to the voice within you. And as you do, I hope you will not forget the moral and ethical lessons of your parents, teachers, friends, this college and, most of all, your own conscience.

But I believe that, by then, you will also have many models of responsible behavior to emulate. It is my intention that Coca-Cola is one of them.

Ends with a reference to his company.

20

The Work of America: A Catholic Perspective on Rebuilding Trust

Bob Wright, NBC

Though the issues of trust and faith are closely linked, very few Fortune 500 CEOs talk about religion. One who does is Bob Wright, vice chairman of General Electric and chairman and CEO of NBC. When he was invited to address Legatus, an organization designed exclusively for top-ranking Catholic business leaders, Wright accepted the challenge of offering a personal and thoughtful perspective from a major Catholic business leader on the corporate scandals and how the Catholic faith might inform one's thinking about this issue. Legatus, started by Tom Monaghan (founder of Domino's Pizza), bills itself as the conduit connecting two powerful realities, the challenge of top-tier business leadership and a religious tradition.

Scoping Document

Event:	Legatus Meeting of Catholic Business Leaders
Theme:	A Catholic Perspective on the Corporate Scandals
Place:	Legatus Tri-State Chapter, New York, New York
Date:	October 29, 2002
Audience:	Approximately 200 Legatus members and guests
Length:	About 19 minutes, 1,744 words

Speech

I have a TV set in my office which monitors CNBC. In recent weeks, it seems as if every time I glanced up from my work, I'd see another image like we just saw on that tape, a corporate executive climbing courthouse steps with his lawyers, or being led away in handcuffs, or getting grilled by Congress.

To make this worse . . . a few years ago, we added a GE stock-price bug to our in-house TV system. As I watched these painful images of some of our nation's

Talking Points

Grabber of an opening.

Plays videotape.

Evokes images we have all seen of CEOs on a "perp walk."

NBC is owned by General Electric, so the speaker is acknowledging a painful fact.

leading executives, I also couldn't avoid seeing how far GE's share price has fallen.

These two things should not be related. Unfortunately, however, to some degree they are. GE is performing extremely well through a very difficult business cycle.

Even as he relates the two things he claims should not be related.

Yet the stock of this company, the bluest of the blue chips, one of the largest, most admired, and, to my mind, most upstanding corporate entities in the country, is being hammered.

Sets up paradox.

It is unfortunate that the breach of trust represented by the scandals at Enron, WorldCom, Adelphia, Xerox, and others, has spilled the boundaries of these individual companies and is now a pressing concern of each and every one of us in the business world.

Yet it is an opportunity as well. An opportunity for all of us to reassess how we run our businesses, how we determine compensation, how we treat our employees, and how we communicate to Wall Street, stockholders, and the general public.

Sets up classic challenge vs. opportunity *equation.*

As tragic as it has been for the employees and investors who have lost livelihoods and life savings to fraud and deceit, I am confident that one day we will be able to look back on this period as a necessary step in securing and preserving the health of American business.

It's a great irony that at the same time that these companies were engaged in wrongdoing, they were never more eager to present themselves as good corporate citizens. Virtually every company, including those that fraud and plunder have left bankrupt, had a company policy with the proper lofty language about their commitment to integrity.

But there is a difference between words and deeds. Arthur Andersen, for example, hired an ethics expert in 1995 to create a corporate-ethics consulting practice for the firm. Unfortunately, the ethics programs she developed for clients were never implemented by her employer. And when she tried to suggest that Andersen adopt some of her programs, she was rebuffed.

Offers concrete example that names names.

Enron put its corporate slogan on coffee mugs, T-shirts, and a huge banner hanging in corporate headquarters: Respect, Integrity, Community, Excellence—RICE for short.

A mnemonic like RICE can be very effective in helping the audience remember a list.

Enron, in fact, was, on the surface, doing everything you could ask of a corporation, and being praised by the public. Enron spent three years on the list of 100 Best Companies to Work for in America. It received six environmental awards in 2000 alone. It issued a triple bottom-line report. Kenneth Lay gave speeches at conferences on ethics.

At the same time, as we know, the foundation was seriously rotten. This was the same company whose board twice voted to suspend their own ethics code and conflict-of-interest rules. If there is one thing our faith teaches us, it is that integrity and morality are internal qualities, and have nothing to do with how well you are dressed or how many awards you've received or how attractive everyone thinks you are.

Contrasting statements.

We all can rationalize what went wrong. At Enron, as at other companies, there was an intense drive to meet the numbers, spurred on by analysts focusing on earnings at the expense of other measures of financial health, and by executives focusing on short-term movements in share price instead of on building viable companies.

There is a whole range of structural issues in the financial markets that encouraged companies to throw good sense, decency, and ethics out the window in their frantic scramble to meet their revenue goals. At Enron, where 60 percent of employees held stock options, and where the real-time stock price was on display for employees even in the elevators at work, the drive to meet the numbers was deep indeed.

Don't misunderstand me. These are not excuses. I worked for Jack Welch. I know about the pressure to perform. And I know how to motivate my division heads to perform. But I know, too, that integrity— whether of a company or an individual—is both invaluable and fragile, and once lost is very hard to regain.

Makes sure he is not being misunderstood. And it's always good to drop the name of your boss, especially if the boss is Jack Welch.

It's about integrity.

Frankly, the tone for a company's ethical culture is set at the top. Employees, consciously or not, will follow the lead of their supervisors and managers. If they see rules being bent, they will bend the rules. And once that process starts, it is very difficult to stop.

Here it works, but starting a point with "frankly" can be confusing because it can cause listeners to wonder if the speaker is being frank in statements not so prefaced.

Enron without a doubt had thousands of good, honest, hardworking employees, who wanted no more than to perform honorably, have the respect of their colleagues, and provide for their families.

Unfortunately, they were working in a company infected with a fatal virus—a virus of bending the rules, looking the other way, and thinking that stock-price performance was the only measure of success. They had failures of leadership, ethics, and governance—a virtual recipe for catastrophe.

Corporate scandals now affect dozens of formerly highly esteemed companies and millions of workers and investors. Beyond the human cost, however, another tragedy of these events is that they have tarnished the image of capitalism and business in our nation.

CEOs are now, believe it or not, less well thought of than lawyers, according to one recent poll. I imagine if you're a lawyer, your comfort in that statistic is outweighed by your dismay at the sizable hit to your stock holdings.

More than 7 out of 10 Americans say they distrust CEOs of large corporations. Nearly 8 out of 10 say they believe that top executives will take "improper actions" to help themselves at the expense of their companies. Big business—not big government—is suddenly seen as a threat.

Offers a memorable statistic.

This is a problem for all of us, who run companies, who recruit the best and brightest young people to work for us, who are actively engaged in the honorable work of American enterprise.

So what do we do about it? How do we, as business leaders, respond to this crisis?

Transition by asking question. Note use of inclusive "we."

The most important step we can take is to rebuild trust. Trust is the engine that drives business. When that is lost, the economic costs are enormous, as we've seen.

We need to rebuild trust among employees. This means making sure that we act like we want our workforce to act. This means rewarding employees who act with exemplary integrity. Rewarding employees who take the ethical stance no matter how

Lists all the ways trust can be rebuilt. Starting each phrase with the common word "We" ties everything together.

unpopular or unprofitable. This also means making it clear that there are consequences for failing to act with integrity, at all levels throughout the company without exception.

We need to rebuild trust among shareholders and on Wall Street. This means addressing the flaws in the system, working with the NYSE on new corporate governance standards to increase the authority of independent directors, ensure their independence, and strengthen the qualifications for members of compensation and audit committees.

"We" reminds audience that they are part of the solution.

We've taken these steps at GE. Recently, in fact, we gathered 32 of our top executives to our training facility in Crotonville for three weeks, charged with a single, focused objective: to study and analyze our company and others, and to present to Jeff Immelt a concrete proposal on what improvements need to be made in our company in the area of corporate governance and social responsibility.

Jeff Immelt is the chairman of General Electric and the speaker's boss.

Our mission is not just to be a great company for investors, but a good company in the eyes of the world.

We've all learned that a business without ethics is a business at risk. And that the slide into a fatal ethical morass is all too easy if top company management is unfocused, or incompetent, or unethical.

In 1981, Pope John Paul II issued his encyclical on the subject of human work. This document presents the position of the Church on work in a way that sheds light, I think, on our current situation.

Appeal to an authority that will resonate with this particular audience of Catholic business leaders.

In the Book of Genesis, Adam and Eve are told by God: "Be fruitful and multiply, and fill the earth and subdue it."

To the Pope, the expression "subdue the earth" has a particular meaning. It refers to the way each and every human being takes part in the giant, ongoing process whereby man uses all the resources of the earth to make things for human use: to grow food, to build housing, to invent new CAT scans, to design improved jet engines, and even to create TV shows—although the Pope doesn't mention NBC specifically.

His point is that "subduing the earth" is a synonym for human work, which is not only fundamentally creative and ethical—but is mandated by God. We can translate those lines from Genesis like this: "Be fruitful and multiply . . . and get to work."

Indeed, the Pope goes further. In the eyes of the Church, the act of work, of contributing your talents to a business, of making things of value, is analogous to the very first act of creation—God's creation of the world.

In other words, when we work, from a theological perspective, we are reflecting the very action of the Creator of the universe. As the Pope writes, "Man's work is a participation in God's activity."

This is worth remembering as we go about our daily lives. Honest and ethical work, no matter how monotonous or alienating, is dignified by God and connected to His creativity.

I think you'll agree that some types of "work" don't fall in this category: accounting fraud, for example. Or setting up sham transactions to book phantom revenue. Or manipulating markets.

Think how the state of American business would be improved if employees everywhere, from top execu-

Making the biblical text relevant and personal. GE makes jet engines; NBC produces entertainment.

Paraphrasing the Pope's argument is easier on the audience than a direct quotation would be.

But don't miss the opportunity to get in one good (and short) quote from the Pope.

Summarizing the theological point . . .

. . . and making it relevant to earlier discussion of corporate scandals.

Transition to conclusion with a far-reaching question. Followed

tives to the mailroom, asked themselves: "Do my actions at work contribute to the creation of value? Does my work reflect the creativity and integrity of God himself? Or is it a sham transaction?"

In the Book of Genesis, each day of creation ends with the words: "And God saw that it was good." My prayer is that one day soon we'll be able to look across corporate America, look at every industry and every company and every boardroom, and be able to say these words as well. Because—fundamentally, essentially, theologically—the work of America is good.

by a series of staccato questions that the speaker hopes his remarks will help answer, although he won't attempt the answers here.

Concludes with a reference to prayer, a topic rarely heard from the CEO podium. Unity is preserved as the final words of the speech echo the quote from Genesis and also give the title ("The Work of America") a theological resonance, as is appropriate for the audience.

Speeches on Diversity

Diversity is one of those words that can mean different things to different people. In fact, it has one very simple and unambiguous meaning: variety. Very few people are against variety. Today, most people accept that organizations make better decisions when managers have the benefit of the experience of people from different backgrounds and perspectives. When speakers get in trouble, it's over the means they endorse in trying to achieve the benefits of diversity. Business speakers need to understand that the word *diversity* conjures up for some people a feeling of unease and threat. Nevertheless, business leaders cannot shy away from the issue. For that reason, when addressing diversity in the workplace, an effective diversity speech:

- Articulates strong personal commitment to diversity
- Employs "I" statements while emphasizing a communal voice
- Anticipates that some members of the audience will be skeptical
- Condemns racism, sexism, and all other barriers to equality
- Does not shy away from the challenges
- Offers specific initiatives for advancing diversity
- Appeals to moral arguments
- Reports positive results while not shying away from the work that remains to be done
- Ends on a hopeful note

21

It Is Payback Time for American Business: Reaffirming Affirmative Action from a Market-based Perspective

Harry C. Stonecipher, Boeing

In this address to the National Action Council for Minorities in Engineering (NACME), Boeing's chairman and CEO Harry Stonecipher delivers a personal message about the need for greater minority enrollment in the nation's engineering schools. The speech mixes statistics with personal narrative to make the case that increasing such enrollment isn't just good public policy, it's in the self-interest of engineering-based companies like The Boeing Company.

Scoping Document

Event:	National Action Council for Minorities in Engineering Summit
Theme:	The 21st Century Workforce
Place:	Washington, D.C.
Date:	June 16, 1998
Audience:	Approximately 1,000 engineering students, faculty, media
Length:	About 9 minutes, 913 words

Speech	Talking Points
Give me a lever . . . and a place to stand . . . and I will move the world." So said Archimedes.	*Starts speech with familiar quote from Archimedes.*
There are many kinds of leverage—not just physical or mechanical, but moral and social, personal and political, financial and economic. Every one represents a means by which the few become capable of lifting the many.	

That is something that Dr. George Campbell and others who serve this organization understand very well. You have demonstrated your mastery of the concepts of leadership and leverage again and again over the past 25 years.

Ties in concept of leverage to theme of address.

The National Action Council for Minorities in Engineering was founded in 1974 following an event like this one at the National Academy of Engineering. It began as a coalition of leaders from government, academia and business who saw a need for positive action in creating greater opportunities for minorities inside the profession.

Tonight is an occasion for celebrating a quarter of a century of progress under NACME's leadership. It is also a time for rethinking old strategies, for brainstorming . . . and for considering new challenges.

Celebration matched with challenge.

Let us begin by recognizing how far we've come . . . and how far we have yet to go.

Try to start with genuine accomplishments to build hope and confidence.

In 1974, African Americans, Latinos and American Indians made up a grand total of one percent of the engineering workforce. One Percent!

Today minorities account for about 10 percent of all Bachelor of Science and Engineering graduates at U.S. colleges and universities.

Good use of statistics: concise and not too much.

No fewer than 6,700 out of roughly 70,000 non-Asia minority engineers today obtained their degrees with the help of NACME scholarships.

By any yardstick, there is still a great shortage of people from minority groups within the engineering profession. NACME is reaching out to groups that make up 28.5 percent of the population and a third of the birth rate. Notwithstanding the progress that has been made, less than six percent of the engineering workforce of today comes from these groups.

Some people would say: What is wrong with this? Should every profession, every career path, precisely reflect the population distribution?

Asks a question on the lips of many in the audience.

In his address to the NACME Forum last year, Dr. Campbell addressed that very question. He pointed out a crucial difference between the relatively small number of minority engineers and—as a counter-point—the small number of white male basketball players in the NBA. There is a clear "legacy of exclusion" on the one side. Whites have had every opportunity to compete in basketball from grade school on up.

Makes the distinction.

Let me add a couple of thoughts from my own perspective.

Speaking from personal experience is preferred.

As the president of an engineering-based company that is one of this country's largest exporters, I know that I cannot afford to compete with one hand tied behind my back—and that is the situation when we as a nation conspicuously fail to tap much of the intellectual and creative potential of large segments of the population.

This is a long and complex phrase, yet its artful structure makes it work. In general, this phrase and others like it in this speech might work even better in shorter phrases that communicate one idea at a time.

We need great engineers, and we need to draw them from every group.

Second, as someone who went to college on a "Grandma scholarship," which is to say, on the savings my grandmother had accumulated as a school teacher in Tennessee hill country, I know something about the value of an engineering or science degree (mine was in physics) to someone who comes from a less-than-affluent background.

A degree in engineering or science is a bootstrap that eliminates poverty by pulling up multiple generations of people. Like many of my friends, I was lucky. I grew up in a family that prized books and learning. From first grade on, I went to schools that were rigorous, disciplined and, in their own way, caring. Every child in this country should have those advantages. But we all know that is, emphatically, not the case.

The $64,000 question is: What are we going to do about it?

An implicit challenge to the audience. Less direct than: "What are you going to do about it?"

The original coalition that NACME began with in 1974 is still intact—and, indeed, bigger and better than ever.

Today, we see a continuing backlash against affirmative action programs in courts and legislatures around the country. At Boeing, we are strongly opposed to any measures that reduce the national commitment to hiring and promoting people from minority groups.

Continued use of "we."

At the same time that we do battle against a variety of measures aimed at rolling back affirmative action, we should recognize that today's world is awash with new possibilities for progress.

Companies everywhere are looking to become more creative and entrepreneurial.

That is certainly what we are trying to do at Boeing Company.

Ties it back to Boeing.

We are tying Boeing scholarships more closely to summer internships with the clearly understood goal of having the inside track on hiring outstanding graduates.

In addition to supporting NACME with $640,000 in giving over the years, we are active with NACME in a wide variety of projects aimed at school reform and insistence on high academic standards for all students at the K–12 level.

In a sense, it is payback time for American business.

Short statement like this indicates transition to conclusion.

Lists a number of Boeing initiatives (omitted).

Concepts such as empowerment and self-directed work teams have roots in the Civil Rights campaigns of the '50s and '60s. So, too, does the basic, activist idea that big organizations are capable of large-scale change; and that people, even within the bowels of a big organization, can determine their own destinies.

In closing, then, I would like to quote the eloquent words of Martin Luther King. As he put it so well, "The greatest progress we have made . . . and the greatest progress we have yet to make . . . is in the human heart."

An example of closing a speech with a powerful quotation.

22

Women to the Rescue: A Business Imperative

Mary Kramer, Crain's Detroit Business

There's good advice for women in this speech about mentoring, being mentored, and performing. Mary Kramer is vice president and associate publisher, Crain's Detroit Business, *the Motor City's leading business publication. Here, she comments approvingly on a program designed to advance women's leadership. That program was developed under the leadership of J. Michael Cook, chairman and chief executive officer emeritus of Deloitte & Touche, who had addressed the club earlier.*

Scoping Document

Event:	Economic Club of Detroit's Business Leaders Luncheon
Theme:	Women in the Workforce
Place:	Detroit, Michigan
Date:	February 22, 1994
Audience:	500 business leaders, managers, media
Length:	About 17 minutes, 1,673 words

Speech

We're talking about human resources today so I'm wondering how many people in the room have ever had the experience of having their employer asking you to take a psychological exam to determine your job potential?

We don't use those exams at *Crain's*, but I'll bet you're familiar with the idea.

I have the results of one test right now.

Talking Points

Direct opening can work.

Asking a question draws audience in.

Making this assumption draws audience to speaker.

This particular test is kind of an antique: It dates to 1980. It's not meant to be compared to the more sophisticated tests employers use today. In fact, the ink blots used for this test look a little like World War II Army surplus. So, please, if there are HR people in the room today and you don't like what I say about the test, no cards or letters; it's old.

This test measured creativity, analytical thinking, judgment and other traits. At best, a manager can use these tests to play to an employee's strengths when making job assignments. At worst, you can use them as a filter. Oh sure, you can use them to prevent those little mistakes like you might not promote Jack Kevorkian to chief anesthesiologist.

Wisecrack here is fairly edgy, although it can be defended on the grounds of locality: Dr. Jack Kevorkian, currently in prison for assisting suicide, was a Michigan celebrity.

But once a manager gets a "lock" on an employee through such a test, he or she may never see potential beyond what's on the test scorecard.

On this particular test, the psychologist met with the employee in person before sending that scorecard back to the employer. There was some bad news for the employee. The test showed a lack of creativity, a tendency to suppress imagination because of a conflicting desire to be conventional.

Perhaps most damning was this assessment: This employee was great on detail work and follow through and would make some lucky manager a wonderful subordinate. But she would NOT be a leader; she didn't have the traits to be a leader.

If you haven't guessed it already, that test was mine.

I took it years before I met my current boss, Keith Crain. Fortunately, he was more interested in my track record as a journalist and his own gut

The speech is about opportunities for women, but this is the first indication of the

feeling—I think they call it INTUITION in women—than in my interpretation of ink blots.

Keith had a gut feeling in 1985 when he created *Crain's Detroit Business*. Even though his CEO-type friends told him he was nuts to start a business publication that didn't cover the Big 3 in Detroit, he had a vision that "there's more to Detroit than just cars."

Because he refused to believe the conventional view of Detroit as a one-industry town, *Crain's Detroit Business* today is a thriving publication with 148,000 readers every week.

Like Keith Crain, Mike Cook scanned the business horizon and saw not only what was there, but what was missing from the big picture. Women. Women were missing from the firm.

Then, like Keith, he and his company did what leaders often do. He took a chance.

Needless to say, I applaud them.

But what impresses me most about the Deloitte & Touche program is not just their commitment but the timing.

Like the other Big Six accounting firms, Deloitte & Touche expects to become a smaller firm in this decade. That's not a goal, but it's a prediction based on business trends and how technology and automation have affected their industry.

And it fascinates me that one of the tools they'll use to increase profitability and productivity in the face of this potential loss in "womanpower."

topic. Probably should appear earlier.

Now zeroes in on the theme.

They'll increase the number of female partners in their firm. They'll teach men and women to work effectively together. And they're listening to what the talented women who are still in the firm are telling them about the ways the business needs to change if they want to keep them on staff.

Professional women, after all, juggle a lot of commitments.

Now Deloitte & Touche is trying to juggle all that, too.

Rule of three.

For me, there is something quite delightful in the thought that these firms think there might be something to this "women thing." Certainly, Deloitte & Touche believes its future hinges on its ability to involve women in every level of activity.

Bringing the speech back to personal experience.

Imagine that: Women to the rescue!

States title of speech.

Of course, women can't rescue any firm or industry just because of the biological gift of femininity.

But what we can do is provide points of view that may be unique to the female experience. Ways of thinking that actually might help the bottom line.

When people ask me about my job, I use words like "cheerleader" and "traffic cop" to describe the management parts of it.

And I think some women were not excited to be at Deloitte & Touche. The firm's own task force found there were three principal reasons for why women were leaving the firm at a rate higher than men. In the words of the press release, it's because of "the general environment," "perceived obstacles of

Reference to recent news as a transition statement.

advancement," and "the need to balance multiple commitments in their lives."

I would like to translate that into the language of the Ladies' Locker Room, and the three reasons sound more like this: "I don't like it here;" "I'm not getting anywhere;" and "Life's too short for this . . . fill-in-the blank . . . I'm out of here!"

So I say bravo to Deloitte & Touche for doing something, for examining themselves and making the company the kind of place a woman wants to hang her briefcase.

Informal way to heap praise.

Now, what about the rest of us?

Transition by asking a question.

I think it can be profitable for any company—maybe every company—to re-examine policies regarding female employees. Who knows? Maybe it's like air bags. Auto companies resisted air bags initially—the seatbelts were plenty good enough; and then they found out they could sell more cars if they had more air bags.

There are lessons here businesses of any size can learn from. I'd like to discuss three for the entire audience and then just one for the women here today.

Introduces three lessons, as way of organizing speech. Better to name the lessons and then drill down.

The first lesson is: You don't have to be a Big 6 accounting firm or a *Fortune* 500 company to get in on this "woman thing."

Lesson number 1.

Many of us, myself included, have succeeded because someone took the time to help our careers. They call it mentoring nowadays. That can be a scary word.

Speakers do well to ally with audience at every opportunity.

Other advice: I couldn't be a buddy to the former peers I suddenly had begun to manage. These mentors are the people I'd call if I had a tough management problem, maybe one about hiring or firing.

I am very grateful to the people who offered advice. I also was never afraid to ask for it. Mentoring works both ways.

Everyone in this room could be a mentor without having a big program or a high-price consultant. You can return to your workplace today, look around, and ask yourself honestly which quality employees are outside the loop. Think about a bright woman who has worked hard but isn't a star. Invite her to a business breakfast or lunch. Think of a way to include her in a new project or team plan.

And that's the second lesson. We must use imagination, not stereotypes or old ink blots to evaluate our employees and their potential.

Lesson number 2.

We in the media share some responsibility for the creation and destruction of stereotypes. If every car you see on the street is a green car, and every car shown by the print or electronic media is a green car, it would be a little tough for you to believe that you could own a red car, or that red cars actually win races.

A third lesson is in the examples we've been seeing—and publishing—of daughters who have taken over businesses previously run by their fathers.

Lesson number 3.

Detroit has plenty of privately owned, closely held businesses. Twenty years ago, many CEOs who also happen to be fathers would never dream of asking their daughters to come into the business. Today it's a little more common. Sometimes it's a daughter with the aptitude and the desire, not the son, who's

asked to step into the father's shoes. And those are
tough calls. I know because I grew up in a family
business that went through just such a difficult
transition.

Adds a personal note to the speech.

And I think we'll know we're really making progress
on this front when the next wave of family succession
comes along and it's mother-daughter or mother-son
transitions!

So much for the general lessons. Now, one word for
women in the audience today.

For a woman or a man to succeed in business, there
is one rule that carries across the board: If you want
the rewards, you've got to do the work. Just because
Deloitte & Touche has a program for women doesn't
mean all women are guaranteed a partnership.
They've got to perform.

Transition from the general lessons to the focus on women.

But what women may have especially overlooked
because it's subtle is that while you have to do the
work, you do not necessarily have to do all the work
yourself.

To be successful in business, a woman must learn to
assemble her own personal success team.

Women must begin to learn to create their own personal success teams: not only the professional skills
we purchase from accountants, attorneys and others,
but the personal relationships that expand our understanding of ourselves, our jobs and our communities.
Those personal and professional networks can help
you define and reach your goals.

Your network is more than a safety net into which
you can gently fall; it's guide wires and ropes with

Memorable way of imagining the safety net.

which you can lift yourself up. And who knows? You might be able to lift a few other people along the way. I think *that* is real power.

We're making progress. Not long ago, I'll bet that some male executive representing the firm could have spoken alone on this platform about the subject: "Women: A Business Imperative" and no one would have raised an eyebrow or thought it a little strange to have a man talking about that alone.

Hopeful conclusion.

Today, I hope it would have been obvious to you, the audience, what was missing at the podium . . . a woman's point of view.

Smart move to end speech with a reference to "women" in the air.

23

Embrace Diversity: Do the Right Thing

Bill Stasior, Booz Allen Hamilton

The chairman and CEO of Booz Allen Hamilton delivered these remarks for the 1998 Diversity Awards, September 17, 1998. The speech mixes poetry, quotations, and personal exhortation to inspire employees to action in the service of embracing diversity. The theme is to get employees not only to "think different" but to "do different."

Scoping Document

Event:	Booz Allen Hamilton awards event
Theme:	Embracing Diversity
Place:	Company headquarters, McLean, Virginia
Date:	September 17, 1998
Audience:	Employees, management, and guests
Length:	About 5 minutes, 529 words

Speech

It's been an incredible evening . . . it's also getting late. So, I want to assure you that I'll be brief, but I do have something important to say.

It's about "doing the right thing."

Many of you have heard me talk about this with respect to our core values of excellence in our work, respect for each other, and inclusion . . . listening to each others' ideas as we debate the important issues of the day.

Today, I'd like to talk about "doing the right thing," but in a different context—one that relates specifically to the issue of diversity.

Talking Points

Promising a quick speech is good . . . now keep the promise.

Announces theme.

Defines context in terms of diversity.

It's important to recognize that doing the right thing is a lot more than not doing the wrong thing.

This is especially true when it comes to diversity.

I believe a lot of people in general—and a lot of people at Booz Allen—are not doing the wrong thing. That is:

Challenges employees to do better by phrasing the negative.

They don't knowingly discriminate in hiring or promotions . . .

Stronger would be to use "we" instead of "they."

They don't make racist or sexist remarks . . .

They don't hate people who are different . . .

But, I believe far fewer people are really "doing the right thing":

Here's the main challenge.

Making a real effort to hire and promote those who are different . . .

Including diverse staff members in their lunch and after-hours get-togethers . . .

Mentoring women and people of color . . .

Martin Luther King, Jr. put it this way: "We will have to repent in this generation not only for the words and actions of the bad people—but for the appalling silence of the good people."

Transition by quotation. The author of the quote is obviously pertinent.

A very confrontational tactic, but it fits here.

Think about it—

If we're really doing the right thing, then supporting diversity must change from a passive concept . . . to an ACTIVE concept!

Here's how he wants employees to change.

The men and women we're honoring here tonight with Booz Allen's Diversity Award, did a lot more than refrain from doing the wrong thing.

They went out of their way to foster diversity:

Here the use of "they" is appropriate.

They devoted great time, effort, and spirit to mentoring staff . . .

The rhythm with these items is very compelling.

They found new opportunities for colleagues . . .

They helped them succeed . . .

They helped them feel like they belong. . .

In turn, we need to ask ourselves:

He finally uses the "we."

Do I support mentoring? Or do I mentor?

Sets up a pair of questions that repeats to good effect.

Do I support diversity? Or do I play an active role in organizations and efforts that foster diversity?

Do I support equal employment opportunity? Or do I insist on seeing a diverse set of candidates for my job openings?

In every case employees understand he wants them to favor the first course.

Do I support equal rights for women, and the disabled, and gays and lesbians? Or do I get involved with programs that will make a difference in the quality of their life?

I came across a poem that captures this very well:

Emphasizes message with a poem that reinforces the key points.

Do more than belong, PARTICIPATE.
Do more than care, HELP.
Do more than believe, PRACTICE.
Do more than be fair, BE KIND.

> Do more than forgive, FORGET.
> Do more than dream, WORK."

This is really our challenge as I see it: To go beyond our good intentions and to make good things happen.

Conclusion starts here.

As we leave tonight, and think about all the things we've heard and learned during the course of this evening, I ask you to . . .

The speech is really coming to an end. Audiences need such cues when the evening draws late.

Do the Right Thing.

Short series of statements draws the speech to an effective close.

Make it an active, (not a passive) commitment.

The Apple Computer ads say, "Think different."

I challenge us to "Do different."

PART 3

Major Announcements and Handling Crises

CHAPTER 6

Speeches for Business Downturns, "Belt-Tightening," and Company Crises

Nobody likes bad news. Not the bearer, not the recipient. One of the toughest challenges for a business leader is to deliver bad news. But "Job One" for such a leader is to be a clear communicator regardless of the circumstances. So leaders who want workers to take them at their word in good times had better choose their words wisely during times that are bad.

The first responsibility of the leader of an organization is to stop the injury, protect life and property, and take control of the situation. The second responsibility, and no less important, is to say the right words. Communicating an effective message is part of crisis management, but it is much more, for many crises are entirely or in large part the consequence of mishandling the communications.

The best way to deliver bad news is one on one. But leaders of large organizations rarely have that luxury. Everyone is looking to you for the correct information. The rumor mill has been working overtime, and it's likely that the general estimation of the situation is even worse than reality. Uncertainty is high, and that creates anxiety. Most of all, the troops need hope. To incorporate these qualities into a speech or remarks in which you must deliver bad news, the following guidelines will help.

- Say it straight. Get right to the point. Announce up front that you have some unpleasant, unfortunate, disappointing, or disturbing news. The right words? Simple: "I have some bad news for you" (see below for alternative phrases).

- Say it first. The bad news is yours. Don't let someone else tell it. Not only does saying it first give you credibility, it lets you shape the message.

- Say it all. Don't try to be selective in the bad news. It'll come out eventually, so get it over with.

- Avoid euphemisms. Don't say "workforce adjustments" when you mean people are getting laid off. If you have something specific to say, use specific words.

- In opening your speech, avoid "softeners" such as "I'm sorry to have to tell you . . ." or "I'm afraid that . . ." It's better to just say it.

- If the news is coming as a shock to the audience, be prepared for an emotional reaction. Legitimize emotions but don't get emotional yourself. The team needs to know that you are thinking clearly about the problem so they can do the emotional work they need.

- Forgive yourself for being the bearer of bad news. You are not the cause of their distress . . . reality is.

- Put yourself in the listener's place. What information will they want?

- Put the crisis in perspective. Try to define the extent of the crisis in terms of place and time.

- If possible outline an approach to handling the crisis.

- Ask for help.

- Conclude by reaffirming your hope for the future and your request for mutual commitment.

There are some alternatives to starting a speech with, "I have some bad news for you." Here's a portfolio of alternate openings:

- I've asked everyone here to report to the community on a very important question. What will happen to us? It's in the spirit of community that I give you this answer.

- Let me outline the situation as I see it and what I propose as the steps necessary for us to recover. We're in a tight spot, but make no mistake, we have successfully navigated much tougher ones.

- The time has now come for us to rely on each other like never before.

- Despite our setbacks, I am confident that, together, we will overcome this downturn and still accomplish all the goals we have set for ourselves.

- The present situation makes unprecedented demands on us all. But knowing you as I do, and having watched you handle bigger setbacks, I am confident that we are more than equal to the challenge.

- Our organization needs the combined effort and intelligence and hopefulness of everyone in this room.

- We have a choice to make: We can lead or we can watch. We can react or we can take a number of proactive business steps starting right now.

- The next period will be demanding, of that there should be no doubt. I don't want to diminish the sacrifices we all will have to accept. But by working together, we will find satisfaction in resolving the difficult issues that confront us.

- I am here to speak to all of you about the recent events that threaten our organization.

- This evening's news will include a report on our company, and I wanted you to hear it from me first. As some of you have heard . . .

- People throughout the community are hurting today because of my decision to shutter the _____ facility. There is no escaping the hard times that come with the loss of ___ jobs. I made the decision, so I wanted you to hear the news from me.

24 The Chrysler Odometer Scandal

Lee Iacocca, Chrysler

In 1987, a scandal erupted when it was revealed that Chrysler Corp. managers had a quality control policy of disconnecting the odometers of some cars, driving them around for up to 100 miles, and then selling the cars as new to unsuspecting customers. Chrysler was also accused of repairing cars that were damaged in accidents and then selling them as new. When the press found out about it, Chrysler and Lee Iacocca were pilloried and investigated. Two Chrysler executives were indicted. Consumer advocate Ralph Nader called for massive money reparations. Dealers reported a fall-off in customer confidence. It fell to a chastened Chrysler chairman Lee Iacocca to manage the crisis. In a press conference on July 1, 1987, he did just that, confronting the issue directly, calling Chrysler's actions "dumb" and "stupid," and taking personal responsibility for cleaning up the mess.

Scoping Document

Event:	News conference
Theme:	Apologizing for the odometer scandal
Place:	Detroit, Michigan
Date:	July 1, 1987
Audience:	News media; Chrysler executives, employees, and dealers; industry analysts
Length:	About 9 minutes, 877 words

Speech

Good afternoon to all of you. I should start by saying that I've had better weeks. I feel a little older than I did a week ago—by at least a couple of years in the last 30 days.

In the past month, I paced the field at the Indy 500 and the Monte Carlo Grand Prix—but back home, I'd say the field got out ahead of me. But after 41

Talking Points

Candid admission that the speaker feels bad about the bad news.

Admission that he lost control, but then puts the problem in context.

years in this business, you learn to take the bitter with the sweet.

As you all know, last week Chrysler was charged with violating the law because of the way we used to conduct our overnight testing program. We'll deal with those legal charges in court, and at the proper time.

Brings everyone up to speed on the issue.

But we've got a much more immediate problem, and that problem we're going to handle today!

Announces the objective of the speech.

Our big concern is for our customers, the people who had enough faith in Chrysler to buy a vehicle from us. These charges, and the press reports about them, are causing some of those customers to question that faith, and we simply cannot tolerate that. If we did something to cause them confusion and concern about the quality of the vehicle they bought, then we're going to fix that right now!

Starts with customers.

Note use of "we."

And by the way, we did do something to have them question their faith in us—two things, in fact.

A clear acceptance of responsibility.

The first was *dumb*. We test-drove a small percentage of our cars with the odometers disengaged and did not tell the customers.

Describes the mistakes in harsh but endearing language.

The second went beyond dumb and went all the way to *stupid*. A few—and I mean a few—cars were damaged in testing badly enough that they probably should not have been sold as new.

"Probably" wasn't Iacocca's choice of words. It's a "weasel word" injected by the lawyers.

These are mistakes that we will never make again, period!

Makes a firm promise.

The only law we broke was the law of common sense.

That's unforgivable, and we've got nobody but ourselves to blame.

Again accepts blame.

But let me set the record straight before I tell you what we're going to do for those customers.

That was the dumb part.

Makes a distinction between two mistakes and focuses on what he considers the bigger mistake.

. . .

The stupid part was fixing and selling a few cars that were damaged in testing, and that maybe shouldn't have been sold. Everybody fixes minor damage, of course. Nobody scraps a $15,000 car for a $15 ding.

Makes sure there's no mistake about what he considers the bigger no-no.

How many cars? Our records show 72 cars that were damaged in the testing. We only sold as new 40 of those, the other 32 were scrapped or sold used at an auction. These numbers hardly establish a pattern of abuse. We don't run a bump and paint shop around here!

Puts the error in context.

Does this sound a little defensive?

Now again, no excuses! Maybe the car shouldn't have been sold as new, even if there was nothing wrong with it. For sure, customers should have been told. It was damaged and repaired—that's where we let the customer down.

If it does, he takes it back. "Maybe." There's another weasel word.

I'm damn sorry it happened, and you can bet it won't ever happen again. And that's a promise.

It's "I" now, no longer "we." A most direct statement of responsibility and a promise.

Believe it or not, we're a helluva lot harder on ourselves than any federal prosecutor or anybody else. If we've had even one case where we sold a car that we shouldn't have, then we violated the trust of every customer. At least that's the way I choose to see it.

Here's what we're going to do.

. . .

This is not a product recall. Hell, the only thing we're recalling here, is our integrity.

So that is what we're doing for our customers. I'd like you to do something for them, too.

I started out by saying that I've had a bad week. Well, a few of you have had a bad week, too.

I don't mind the cartoons of good old Lee, the used car salesman—hell, I laughed at them myself. Well, I cried a little too. I'll take the shots—fair or unfair.

But I do mind—one helluva lot—the stories that have caused our customers more concern than they need to have. Some now think that all we do around here is joy riding in the cars every night and then roll back the odometers in the morning.

We don't do that, never did, and you know it.

We're bending over backward to be fair to our customers. But those people are also your customers—your readers and viewers—so I hope you'll be fair to them, too.

This thing is crying out for a little perspective.

We're talking about two percent of our cars being tested.

We're talking about an average of 40 miles.

We're talking about a tiny fraction of them being damaged, and mostly very minor damage.

Transition to a long section where Iacocca outlines a specific set of policy changes (omitted).

He ends that policy section with this conclusion statement.

Transition.

Back to "I" indicates a more personal tone.

Iacocca is referring to some brutal newspaper editorial page cartoons.

Focus on customers.

Now he's talking to the news media.

Now in persuasive mode, trying to convince the media of his position. He uses short series of sound bites.

Note rhythm of the sound bites, concluded by the "and."

And we're talking about an even tinier fraction of them being sold when maybe they shouldn't have been.

Did we screw up? You bet. We're human. Sometimes people do dumb things. But all this nonsense about "Where's the pride?"—well, we never lost it. Because we're proud of the huge quality improvements we've made at Chrysler.

Transition question followed by a direct statement of responsibility.

Finally, after all we've been through here at Chrysler, we sure as hell aren't going to compromise everything we've accomplished by intentionally mistreating the customer in the way the stories in the past week have portrayed.

You know us better than that; at least I hope you do. And I sure have to hope that our customers do.

Concludes, as it began, with focus on customers.

I Am Here Today to Apologize to All of American Airlines' Employees

Donald J. Carty, American Airlines

After five years at the helm of American Airlines, CEO Donald J. Carty paved the way for his own downfall. He negotiated $1.8 billion in pay concessions from the unions, threatening all the while to take American into bankruptcy. But as he was beating the drums for concessions from the employees, he failed to disclose a little known program designed to guarantee the pensions of the top executives in case of bankruptcy. Employees have no similar guarantees. To add insult to injury, the program put the top executives in line for hefty bonuses. The resulting firestorm of criticism came from the rank-and-file as well as the board of directors. To his credit, Carty immediately realized his blunder and offered contrite and apparently sincere apologies. As apologies from CEOs go, Carty's remarks are a model of clarity. He not only acknowledges what he did wrong and accepts personal responsibility, he offers a form of restitution by rescinding the pension plan and bonuses. What he didn't do was take personal responsibility for his conduct by offering his resignation. The directors of AMRCorp, the parent company of American Airlines, felt the breach of trust was insurmountable. On April 25, 2003, the board forced Carty to resign.

Scoping Document

Event:	News conference
Theme:	Apology for misleading employees and board
Place:	Dallas, Texas
Date:	April 21, 2003
Audience:	News media, employees, executives, aviation analysts
Length:	About 14 minutes, 1,405 words

Speech

I am here today to apologize to all of American Airlines' employees, as well as our union leaders, for my mistakes in judgment that have been the cause of so much upset over the past several days. And I will do that.

But first, I want to acknowledge the passing of Bob Baker last night. Bob was an extraordinary person who made countless contributions to American's success for more than 30 years. He was also a great friend to many at American and throughout our industry, and he will be sorely missed. Our thoughts and prayers are certainly with his family at this time.

Now, turning to the business at hand . . .

Today we are at an important crossroad in American's ongoing march toward survival. We've come this far because everyone has pulled together to make the tough choices and do what is necessary to keep this great company of ours out of bankruptcy.

Our union leaders stepped up to the plate by quickly hammering out consensual agreements. Our unionized employees stepped up to the plate by ratifying them. Indeed, all of our employees, union and nonunion alike, did what was necessary to help avoid bankruptcy. And then, I stumbled.

You know, the world's largest airline doesn't do things halfway. When we do something, we do it bigger and better than anyone else. Together, we did

Talking Points

When you need to apologize, just do it.

Carty spells out what he did wrong.

Sometimes leaders must interrupt their own self-destruction to attend to something even more important. As these events played out, a cherished company executive died. The death of a senior member of the executive team demands acknowledgment, and it puts the other matters at hand into context.

These transitions can be awkward.

Offers a little context for the situation.

Acknowledges the concessions of the unions.

"Stumbled" may be a little weak. "Screwed up" is how Lee Iacocca would say it (see Speech 24).

Injects a little humor by way of acknowledging that his was a huge stumble.

what has never before been done—and many thought couldn't be done. We delivered the largest consensual savings in U.S. history.

And then I made a mistake and, of course, it was a big one.

Therefore, my apology, and the actions I take to demonstrate my commitment to the employees of this airline, must be big as well.

A big mistake calls for a big apology.

So, today I am again reaching out to our union leaders and employees in the most public way I know how.

First, I want to offer my sincere and most heartfelt apology to the men and women of this airline and to the people and communities we serve. It was never my intent to mislead anyone, and I hope my apology can begin to heal the hurt I have caused.

Promises multiple actions.
Action number 1 is to apologize.

Second, I want to restate that we have canceled any and all retention payments for company officers. The retention payments are gone—period. I hope this is a tangible demonstration of my commitment to respect the feelings of our employees and to do what's right by them.

Action number 2.

And third, I want to let you know that I have just met with our union leaders to fully brief them about our compensation policies and practices and to completely answer any and all questions they may have about them. Clearly, I should have done this sooner.

Action number 3.

I know that our union leadership must have complete confidence in the fact that the sacrifices are indeed shared and that there are no more surprises. They deserve the truth and so do our employees.

And, so that I don't repeat my past communications mistakes, I have pledged to brief them on all these matters in the future.

In fact, the controversy that is swirling around us today can be laid squarely on my misjudgment in communicating the facts about our company's executive retention programs.

Again takes responsibility.

While I did brief our union leaders on the very serious issues the company faced in keeping key executives, and my need to address it, I failed in not giving them the full details of our plan. I also fell short in conveying to my management team and our spokespeople that I had not fully briefed our union leaders on my discussions.

Explains his failure so everyone knows that he gets it.

Throughout all this, the AMR board operated well within all standard corporate guidelines to address a very real and serious retention problem. So while the board's actions were proper, my subsequent handling of the issues was not. Because I failed to fully communicate the details in advance, I inadvertently created a perception that there was something improper. I understand that perception is indeed reality, and I'm going to work hard to ensure that our employees' perception about our compensation practices at American matches what I believe to be the reality.

Takes sole responsibility. Heaps praise on board.

"Inadvertently" is a tad defensive.

I hope my apologies, my cancellation of all retention payments, and my commitment to be completely open about these matters—now and in the future—can begin to build a bridge back to the path that allowed us to forge these historic agreements in the first place—a path that promised a new culture of collaboration, cooperation and trust.

His hopes for what the apology will accomplish.

I know that it won't happen overnight, but I am committed to gaining our employees' confidence—a valuable commodity that must be earned, and then re-earned, every single day.

An important building block to that bridge back to trust and confidence is for our union leaders and employees to have full confidence in the fact that the sacrifices they were asked for and agreed to make are indeed shared and that we are all in this together. So I hope my record in this regard speaks more clearly than I obviously have about the full details.

Acknowledges need for trust and confidence.

I did take a 33 percent pay cut, and all members of management have taken pay cuts as well. I have not received a bonus for the past two years; nor have any other members of my officer team. I have declined a bonus for this year, and I did not receive any retention payment or bonus, as some of my counterparts at other airlines did.

Discusses the restitution: what he's going to change.

I'll say this again so there is no misunderstanding: I did not receive any retention payment or bonus.

I also asked that my 2003–2005 performance share grant be canceled and the board did so. And as I said before, given the financial performance of the company, this is as it should be.

So, all in all, my total compensation is down by over 80 percent. I am the lowest paid CEO among the major carriers. I want to make clear, I am in no way complaining. I simply want our employees to be assured that executive compensation at American is in line with—in fact, below—industry standards.

It is important that all the employees who have been asked to share in the sacrifice understand that despite my mishandling of this particular situation, the board has acted responsibly. And I have indeed shared in the sacrifice, and my commitment is real.

We all made the sacrifices necessary to help save this company from bankruptcy because we all knew tens of thousands of lives would be adversely affected if we did not.

Transition to closing using a series of statements prefaced by "we" as if to underscore the point that his continued position at the helm of the company is assumed.

We worked hard and we worked fast because we knew that with the company losing millions every day, and with large debt payments due, we were up against very real deadlines with serious consequences.

The consensual agreements that we forged— together—are necessary to help secure better futures for the people who depend on us.

Emphasizes "together" as a theme.

It bears repeating that my mishandling of the situation at hand notwithstanding, our financial condition has not changed. We still are on the precipice of bankruptcy. That's why we have begun to implement the restructuring measures contained in the ratified agreements. If we don't, we regrettably will have no alternative but to file—something we all worked very hard to avoid because we knew it was not in our employees' best interest to do so.

Moves from personal mea culpa to hard-headed CEO.

The fact is, the precariousness of our financial condition simply can't sustain any action that would delay or prevent the consensual restructuring measures from taking place on schedule.

So, as I stated in my opening remarks—we are at a crossroad. This is a difficult time for our airline—in fact, the most challenging period we have ever faced. To emerge successfully from these trying

Good speeches build in some redundancy to underscore the main points.

times, it is important that our employees know that all are sharing in the sacrifices necessary to secure our future. And that will be the case.

Over the past couple months, our collective efforts to restructure costs have shown to everyone the commitment of the people of American Airlines. They are simply the best. And I join them in letting everyone know— both competitors and customers alike—that American intends to be here for a very, very long time.

In closing, I again apologize to our employees and union leaders, and I ask for their forgiveness. I'll learn from this mistake, and I'll be a better person because of it. And more importantly, American will be a better company for its employees.

A speaker's sincerity can be judged by the last words of the speech. Conclusion by repeating apology and ending, appropriately, with an emphasis not on the individual but on the organization and the employees.

26

Chrysler Shuts a Plant in Kenosha, Wisconsin

Lee Iacocca, Chrysler

The toughest job for a CEO is to announce the closing of a significant factory or plant. Thousands of jobs are on the line, as well as the economic fortunes of an entire community. The stakes are as high as the outpouring of emotions. Chrysler had an 86-year-old plant in Kenosha, Wisconsin, that was deemed too old to renovate, despite much community interest in doing so. When Chrysler announced the plant closing in January 1987, the company's image and Chairman Lee Iacocca's reputation came under fire. Editorials attacked both the company and its management. The Wisconsin governor threatened to sue Chrysler. It was in the heat of that battle that Iacocca journeyed to Milwaukee to address the Kenosha community. His remarks were direct, acknowledging the pain, taking responsibility for the outcome, and daring to challenge the perception of Chrysler as a villain. In Iacocca's speech, Chrysler was also a victim.

Scoping Document

Event:	Community meeting
Theme:	Announcing decision to close Kenosha, Wisconsin plant
Place:	Milwaukee, Wisconsin
Date:	February 16, 1988
Audience:	Community members, local officials, employees and families, media
Length:	About 8 minutes, 774 words

Speech

Good afternoon. Based on some of the things I've read and heard in the last two weeks, there are probably a lot of you who doubted I'd ever show up here in person.

Talking Points

Acknowledges the painful emotion filling the room.

Well, I'm here. It may have taken me too long, but there were good reasons for that; I didn't have a message to deliver, and I didn't have a plan to present. But we've talked to a lot of people—and heard from the people of Kenosha—and we've put a plan together. That's why I'm here today.

Is not afraid to accept the challenge. Explains the delay in making this speech.

Purpose of speech is to announce an economic plan.

Let me say at the outset that I've seen Chrysler raked over the coals for two weeks, and I think some of it has been unfair. Unfair—but understandable.

Tries for a balanced perspective.

In the heat that always follows a plant closing, emotions naturally run high. And I'm an expert on that; I've had to close a lot of plants. It's a lousy time to try and communicate, because people are angry and nobody listens well when they're angry.

Let me start by reminding you that we've said from the outset that we'd not only meet our normal obligations to our workers and the community, we'd go beyond them. We intend to do just that, and I'm here to tell you—and the people of Kenosha—just how we'll do that.

Sets up the agreement.

Makes a promise.

But first, let me repeat that the decision to close the Kenosha plant later this year was a crummy call that we had no choice but to make. We've been through all that. We didn't renege on anything . . . and we didn't break our word to anybody. Time, and the marketplace, just caught up with an 86-year-old plant.

Reviews the facts from Chrysler's perspective.

Is this a bit too defensive?

When you have to make a decision like we did, you're the villain. There's no getting around it. It comes with the territory. Most people don't see it yet, but we're really not villains at Chrysler—we are victims. Not quite as much as those people losing their jobs, but victims nevertheless.

Reframes the argument. Astonishing argument that Chrysler is as much victim as villain.

We're all victims—all of us in this country—of years of unfair trade policies that have flooded our market with foreign products, closed our factories, and put our people on the street. This isn't a Chrysler problem, or a Kenosha problem—it's an American problem.

Now everyone is on the same side.

But it never hits home, does it, until it's your job . . . or the guy's next door . . . or the guy who sits in front of you in church. Until then, it's just a bunch of employment figures or trade numbers in small print at the bottom of the business page.

Well it hit home in Kenosha a couple of weeks ago. For that community, it felt like the world fell in. But it's not just in Kenosha. Right now, even as we stand here, the same thing is going on in:

Norwood, Ohio . . . 4,000 jobs
Hamilton, Ohio . . . 2,500 jobs
. . .

Lists about 20 cities losing plants and jobs. It truly is a national problem.

But let me add that Kenosha was destined to close. Regardless of who owned it—American Motors . . . Renault . . . Chrysler . . . or somebody else. It can't compete anymore; the plant, not the people. It's just happened sooner than we expected.

Setting up support for the Chrysler-as-victim argument.

That's the stark naked reality of the thing. I'm just the messenger bringing the bad news. If you want to beat up on me, okay, but you'd better go to Washington if you want to fix it.

A little defiant here.

Nevertheless, the people in Kenosha are our people . . . and the community has relied for a long time on a plant that is now ours, so we've got a special obligation to help them out.

Backing off and becomes more conciliatory.

We made a mistake with Kenosha, and I'm here to admit it. We are guilty as hell of being cockeyed optimists. And we're paying the price for it now.	*Accepts responsibility. What follows is a long passage on the cause of the problem in a national context.*
I've received a lot of mail from Kenosha. Some of it we can't print. Most of the letters, though, just have a lot of pain, and a lot of worry in them. I wish I didn't have to read them all—but I do.	*Transition to an intensely personal level.*
This one is from John Hosmanek. He is the superintendent of schools. He says 1,905 families with a total of 2,358 kids in his schools are going to be hurt.	*He reads a chunk of the letter. Then talks about other personal stories he's heard.*
Those are the big problems that the people of Kenosha have told us about. And we're gonna do something about them. Starting now. And that's the program I want to outline today.	*Introduces the economic assistance program that Chrysler will offer Kenosha. What follows are details of the program.*
Now, I know that this program won't end the pain, but I sure hope it will start the healing.	*After the details, Iacocca transitions to the conclusion with a kind of rhetoric that was not used earlier in the speech.*
Maybe if we can get people working together to help the Kenosha employees—the company, government, community groups—we can turn off the rhetoric and start helping Kenosha look to the future.	*Ends with a statement of hope for the future.*

27

Crossing the Line:
An Industry About to Fail

Bruce Karatz, KB Home

When an executive needs to confront an organization on the ropes, he or she must walk a fine line. On the one hand, the seriousness of the situation must be spelled out. Ignoring reality in such situations serves no purpose. On the other hand, the executive must take care not to add to the problem by further demoralizing the audience. That is the challenge that Bruce Karatz, CEO of KB Home, a leading home-building company, faced as he examined the state of an industry that was—frankly—failing. Working with speechwriter David Berger, Karatz knew that if he wanted to reach a skeptical audience, he would have to challenge as well as inspire them. The theme they chose was to compare the lagging homebuilders industry with the high-tech industry, perhaps the most successful industry of all time.

Scoping Document

Event:	Homebuilder conference
Theme:	The future of the homebuilding industry
Place:	Las Vegas, Nevada
Date:	November 12, 1999
Audience:	Approximately 2,000 homebuilder professionals
Length:	About 9 minutes, 900 words

Speech

I'd like to tell you a story about an industry. It's an industry we're all familiar with. This industry has got a hip corporate culture that attracts the best and the brightest workers. It's an industry filled with companies that are cutting big deals and acquiring each other at a record pace.

Talking Points

Everybody loves stories. Speaking to over 100 leading home-building CEOs—his peers as well as competitors—Karatz wants to make audience members comfortable.

It's an industry where a company's market share helps determine how successful they'll be. It's an industry that's driven by marketing, and where companies take risks to stay on the cutting edge of the consumer culture.

It's an industry where customer satisfaction can make or break a company. It's an industry where you've got to stay on the leading edge of technology, or you risk being left behind in the blink of an eye.

Now, how many of you think I'm talking about the homebuilding industry? Not too many of you are raising your hands. Now how many think I'm talking about the high-tech industry?

I see a lot more hands.

Asking a question is a gentle way to move an audience past its comfort zone.

He piques the interest of audience members immediately by asking questions and requesting that his listeners raise their hands in response. By forcing his audience to interact with him and each other, Karatz ensures that everyone is paying close attention and not getting bored.

The truth is, I'm talking about both industries. I'm describing where the high-tech industry is today, and where homebuilding will be tomorrow—*if* we want to be considered among America's elite companies.

The "If" is the challenge, implying that success is a matter of will.

Instead of accepting the differences between the tech sector and the homebuilding sector, we should close the gap. All of us talk to our employees about the importance of sharing best practices. Tonight, I want to take a closer look at the best practices of the best tech firms, and see what we can learn.

High-tech firms attract the best and the brightest talent out of college. Yet, it's more than money that's attracting this talent. High-tech firms have created a corporate culture that attracts creative thinkers.

It's not just the casual dress and the team orientation. The most progressive firms offer everything from on-site child care to flex-time to corporate campuses with modern gymnasiums to paid sabbaticals. In exchange for these conveniences and perks, employees at tech firms show a level of corporate commitment that should be the envy of us all.

If we can consistently achieve the kind of productivity and enthusiasm that's seen in the country's leading high-tech companies, it's worth getting rid of those pieces of silk around our necks, offering a few more perks, and delegating more authority to workers half your age.

Technology is also hip because it's where the action is.

Open up the *Wall Street Journal* every day, and it's likely you'll see a report of a new alliance or acquisition between two tech companies. Whether it's At Home and Excite, Netscape and AOL, Yahoo and Broadcast.com, the high-tech industry contracts just as quickly as it expands.

Industry consolidation accomplishes several things. It's designed to give companies access to new and better technology. It brings them the best young minds in the industry. It enables them to extend their brand into different markets. And it gives them the opportunity to cross-promote among different platforms—giving them a broader reach.

He proceeds to challenge all the elements of homebuilding orthodoxy.

Compares the homebuilding industry with America's current corporate darling—the high-tech industry.

The same principles apply to homebuilding, and that's why we think the consolidation trend is going to gather momentum in the years to come.

We've also got to adopt the aggressive marketing approach of the high-tech industry.

From their very beginnings, tech firms understand that it's just as important to achieve "share of mind" as it is to achieve "share of market." That's why start-up tech firms pour every dime they've got into aggressive marketing programs and brand-building campaigns.

I've put together a few high-tech ads for you, and I'd like you to pay attention to what they're selling. It certainly isn't product.

We'll also have to become more aggressive in our customer satisfaction programs. The tech industry has created some of the most innovative customer satisfaction programs around. They've learned the importance of building in customer satisfaction programs in the sales process itself—and not just on the back end.

The technology revolution hasn't just been about consumers. It's also been about companies. The high-tech industry has successfully created a new way of doing business that hasn't been fully captured in the media or Harvard Business School case studies. While many would say what we do and what Bill Gates or Michael Dell do are fundamentally different, I say it doesn't have to be—if we're ready to acknowledge the new rules of business that they've laid down.

Karatz goes on to list all the ways the homebuilding industry can change to more closely mirror the high-tech industry—learning from the best practices of the latter.

Karatz's speech was accompanied by an ongoing stream of visuals. To stress the idea that homebuilders have "got to adopt the aggressive marketing approach of the high-tech industry," he played some high-tech marketing commercials.

After showing the ads—the very nature of which built the audience's excitement and understanding—Karatz continues to emphasize why, to succeed, the homebuilding industry must eventually parallel the trends found in the high-tech industry.

Karatz wants the audience to consider the viability of trying new things and going out on a limb.

But even more motivational is his promise to set an example and take the first step.

In fact, I'm willing to make the ultimate sacrifice. We've been spreading the K&B message to Wall Street, talking about our record sales, our 14 consecutive quarters of earnings growth, and our winning strategy. It hasn't been enough, so we're taking the next step. . . . Kaufman and Broad is changing its name to keep up with the times. . . .

That was news that had yet to be released to the media—and when Karatz revealed the new name and logo to his audience, the reaction was charged and excited, as each homebuilder envisioned the changes that he, too, would soon make.

CHAPTER 7

Speeches Announcing New Strategy

Organizations, more than individuals, can be hard to change. Speeches challenging organizations to stretch their values requires leaders willing to stretch theirs. There are few rules for structuring such a speech, but the following guidelines may help. A speech that effectively gets an organization to challenge its values

- Acknowledges the good work the organization has done to date
- Recognizes that the old ways are no longer effective
- Names the pain and acknowledges how everyone will suffer
- Creates a sense of shared sacrifice: that the speaker participates in the pain
- Articulates a vision of how the new way will be better
- Offers audiences permission to be uncertain
- Uses humor effectively
- Convinces the audience that the speaker is personally committed to the change

28

Announcing a Change in Brand Identity

Michael Eskew, United Parcel Service

In March 2003, United Parcel Service (UPS) went public with its new brand identity. It was a significant moment in the history of the company . . . it was only the third logo change in 97 years of business. The most recent is perhaps the most dramatic rebranding campaign in its history. More than just a logo change, UPS embarked on a coordinated campaign to signal customers that it is more than just a delivery company. The goal of the new campaign? To communicate to customers that it is a mover of commerce, whether that takes the form of packaged goods, information, or funds. Coordinated with a new advertising campaign, the rebranding effort was launched in a speech by Chairman and CEO Michael Eskew. The facelift comes as UPS, still the dominant package delivery company, faces increasing competition from FedEx and others. One of the challenges of the speech was to hold on to the legacy of UPS's past and its shield logo while embracing the move to a new logo and all that it represents.

Scoping Document

Event:	Senior management meeting
Theme:	Change of UPS brand identity
Place:	Company headquarters, Atlanta, Georgia
Date:	March 25, 2003
Audience:	About 250 senior managers at UPS
Length:	About 14 minutes, 1,414 words

Speech

"Determined people make conditions . . . they do not allow themselves to be victims of them."

Talking Points

Given that a link to the past is so critical, it is fitting that the speaker begins with a quotation from a former CEO.

For a man whose wisdom could fill volumes of books
. . . these 14 words just might have been Jim Casey's
crowned jewels.

Jim first said them 56 years ago at the Management
Conference.

*This timeline reminds the
audience of the legacy of UPS.*

A time before most of us were born.

*Speakers makes good use of
pauses.*

And like today, a time of major transition in our
company . . . and in the world of commerce.

*Short sentence fragments gives
a sense of movement . . .
transition.*

Jim used this simple phrase to support an important
point.

That our path to success rests upon:

Names three elements of success.

A clear understanding of what we want to
accomplish ...

*Nowhere is the rule of three bet-
ter demonstrated.*

A clear plan to get us to that destination . . .

And the instincts to know when the time is right to
take action—to make conditions.

Pause.

Like our great company, these powerful words have
stood the test of time.

*Emphasis on time underscores
message of change.*

They have shaped and defined the leadership culture
of UPS.

And they've never been more relevant than right
now.

As I look to each of you . . . the leaders of our
company . . . I too see determined people.

Links the past with the present.

Leaders whose actions and examples have inspired thousands of future leaders.

Stewards of one of the strongest and most respected brands the world has ever known.

"Stewards" connotes a precious thing in the temporary safekeeping of a group of people.

Our brand has endured because those before us had the wisdom . . . and the courage . . . to make changes—and face difficult decisions.

First mention of brand. It won't be the last.

That was their legacy to us.

Pause.

Now . . . it's our time to begin laying the foundation for our own legacy.

Transition to the current challenge.

A big part of that responsibility means ensuring that our brand defines who we are . . . and reflects the times we live in.

As partners we owe this to those who will follow us.

We owe them a UPS conditioned for a climate of continuing success.

When you look at this . . . what do you see?

Slide of old UPS logo.

Strength . . . solidarity . . . and integrity—are just some of the words that come to my mind.

Answers the question.

Beyond the words—are the emotions.

Appeal to emotions. The metaphor of friends taking care of each other.

This is an old friend. A trusted friend.

A friend that has served us and our families well for over 40 years.

It's given us comfort . . . security . . . personal . . . and
professional growth.

It's given us the privilege to serve our customers with
the highest of ideals . . . and the chance to better our
communities.

Pause.

But as strong and as valued as this old friend is . . . it
no longer represents all that we are today . . . nor all
that we can be tomorrow.

The "but" signals another transition.

The time has come to move on.

After more than 40 years of honorable service, it's
time for this old friend to retire with the grace and
dignity it deserves.

Friends retire; logos do, too.

So, today, we're saying "goodbye."

This is also a farewell speech.

But unlike most goodbyes, this is not an ending.

Rather, this is a new beginning.

And a speech of introduction. On the word "this," the old logo dissolves into the new logo.

A bold, determined and re-energized beginning.

Today is a truly historic moment in the history of
UPS.

The insertion of the adverb "truly" avoids the speaker having to say the awkward "an historic moment."

We're telling the world to take a closer look . . .
because we've changed.

Customer needs have changed . . . and the world of
commerce has changed.

A world that expects more than packages from UPS.

It's a matter of customer expectations. Pause.

Make no mistake … we thought long and hard about this.

Just like Jim Casey did when he changed the original logo in 1937 and then again in 1961.

In my office, hanging on the wall, is a painting of a package car bearing that 1937 logo.

Over the past several months, I've studied that picture . . . and reflected on what all the leaders before us must have been thinking.

What they must have been wrestling with to keep our company invigorated, fresh and dynamic.

And I thought about the same questions they must have asked themselves when contemplating significant changes in our company . . . like "why are we doing this?"

In our case today, it's because the world needs to know that we're a much different company than we were in 1961. We're a much different company than we were in 1991 . . . and even 2001.

Worldwide reach. World-class technologies. The broadest and most powerful product portfolio in our industry. The 1961 shield does not portray the here and now of UPS.

Which leads to the next question . . . the timing . . . why now?

Now . . . because this is exactly the time . . . during periods of challenge and regrouping . . . when leadership companies step up to the plate.

The pause signals a transition to a more personal note.

If there is precedent for change, make note of it.

Telling a personal story now.

Pause.

Laying out the case for the change.

Asks question on the mind of everyone listening to the speech.

Starts sentence with the same word that ends the question.

We must invest in the business today to prepare ourselves for sustained growth when the economy corrects itself.

In making big decisions like this we must also weigh some other important factors.

We need to think about our people and this extraordinary culture of ours.

Complete emphasis on "we."

We need to think about the way we measure and reward our people.

We need to think about how we're structured.

And we need to think about our processes—how we get things done.

Over the last several years—during this entire transformation journey—we've addressed each one of these areas.

While there is still work to be done, we've been successful in making the needed adjustments.

But sometimes, conditions call for additional signals of change.

Symbols play a powerful role in communicating transformation—not just where we've come from and who we are today . . . but our vision for the future.

By revitalizing one of the most powerful symbols in business, we're also telling the world, there's more to come. Much more.

Pause.

Before deciding on this exact design, we sketched literally hundreds of different variations.

It was an elaborate exercise in constructive dissatis-
faction . . . Jim's other phrase. He would have been
proud of the deliberation and care we took in craft-
ing this.

As you can see, some things have changed . . . but
we'll never abandon the timeless, rock-solid values
that the shield stands for . . . those enduring beliefs
in serving our customers with integrity, innovation
and excellence.

*Some values will always be pre-
served.*

These values are the alloys that give the shield
strength.

*Is there a nobler, more perfect
word than "alloys"?*

In a few minutes, you're going to see, up close, how
our new shield will be portrayed on our package
cars, aircraft, facilities, uniforms and other items.

And during this time, I want you to keep one
thought in mind. One very important thought.

This is not merely an exercise in changing a logo.

*Caution that a logo change is
not enough: It must be followed
up with action.*

Symbols only go so far.

This is much more than that.

This is about a new mindset . . . a new way of projecting our company . . . our people . . . our capabilities . . . our role in the future of commerce.

This is about a new way of projecting our fundamental promise to our customers—our brand.

*Emphasizes importance of brand
again.*

UPS will remain synonymous with the world's premier package delivery company . . .

*Defines the brand equity to make
sure everyone is on the same
page.*

At the same time, we will be more than that.

We've set our sights . . . and our vision is clear.

We've enhanced our capabilities to be the first-to-market leader in a new and larger industry space.

A marketplace that asks us to "synchronize commerce. . . ."

Moving goods

Topic statement of the new UPS value proposition, conveyed by the rule of three.

Information

And funds. . . .

All designed to streamline our customers' operations . . . and grow their businesses on a global scale.

Pause between thoughts for emphasis.

Being first-to-market in such an important market space—will have very profound and lasting impacts on our brand and our people.

Transition.

Imagine leaving a legacy that gives every UPSer . . . today . . . tomorrow and for the next 96 years . . . even more opportunities to grow and be successful?

Returns to context of the historic tradition being played out.

That's not wishful thinking . . . that's our job.

Jim had it right: Determined people make conditions . . . they don't allow themselves to be victims of them.

Today, we're telling the world—loud and clear—that UPS makes its own conditions.

But we all know that deeds trump words.

No more so than with our people and our customers.

Never has there been a time in our careers when our words and our actions must be more aligned with the direction of our company and our brand.

For some of us, this might require a change in the way we think about our business . . . our strategies . . . and our processes.

And quite frankly, for some of us, change is not always easy.

But it's absolutely necessary.

We're the company's top brand ambassadors.

We must "live" the brand.

Another branding statement.

Our people need to sense this . . . and believe it . . . and own it, themselves.

Our customers need to embrace it.

Their enthusiasm . . . and their acceptance of this change . . . will only be as strong as our own.

Leaders create these kinds of conditions.

And we'll do so with the power of one great company behind us. . . .

The final thoughts the speaker leaves the audience with: "brand," "inspire," and "us." The rest of the speech is just commentary.

. . . with the power of one clear vision to guide us. . . .

. . . and with the power of one incredible brand to inspire us.

29 | On the Hardships of Relocation

John Kador

The CEO of a major organization addressed 200 managers about a major change. The company would be opening a new customer support center in another state that would require the relocation of hundreds of people. In addition, the firm for the first time would institute Saturday hours. The first draft of the CEO's speech basically laid out the changes and talked about the rationale for the decisions. But then the CEO decided he wanted to be less directive. He wanted to lead by getting real buy-in from the managers, not just compliance. It is relatively easy to give orders. It is another thing to earn the loyalty of people so they will follow with enthusiasm. Here is the way the revised speech was delivered.

Scoping Document

Event:	Meeting of branch managers
Theme:	Changes required to staff new customer support center
Place:	Regional management meeting
Date:	Anytime
Audience:	Branch managers and senior executives of the company
Length:	About 3 minutes, 339 words

Speech

At first, I was quite excited about the new customer support center and all the changes, and I assumed you would be, too.

But you have helped me learn an important lesson. There is a way that executives are shielded from the decisions they make on behalf of the organization.

Talking Points

Starts with a very personal tone.

The speaker credits his critics and makes himself vulnerable.

As you know, we have been considering both relocation to another state and opening the branches for a few hours on Saturday for some time.

And I assumed that everyone would see the benefits of these actions.

But as I thought about the impact of these changes, it occurred to me that the relocation did not require *me* to move from *my* home, and in fact, *I* was not going to work any more hours on Saturday than I already do. *My* children are used to my irregular hours, but I know that for many of you, Saturday hours would be a major disruption.

For many of you, an occasional Saturday away from the family will be something new, and certainly these changes will cause some disruption in the family patterns of your staffs.

It also occurred to me that I wasn't going to be telling my staff about moving or working on Saturdays. Rather, I get to address the big issues, while *you* will be conveying the news to individuals and dealing with very specific questions.

Given these thoughts, I quickly realized that you might not be as excited about these moves as I am, even though these changes are for the good of the company and ultimately will create more opportunity for all of us.

So this evening, I want to outline the rationale for the changes, let you know what tremendous effort has gone into the business planning, and speak for just a moment about the impact these changes will ultimately have on our company's growth rate. Then I also want to spend some time discussing the con-

Gets everyone on the same page and cues the audience that this is a "we" speech, not a "you speech."

Acknowledges that the major brunt of the changes will not fall on the speaker.

Continues with highly personal tone, even bringing in his children.

Acknowledges that the executive's circumstances are different than the average employee's.

Acknowledges that although the speaker made the decision, the job of breaking the news falls on his managers.

Gives audience permission to feel ambivalent about the announcement.

Speaker becomes collegial, seeking buy-in, not just compliance.

siderations we went through about the personal impact on you and your families. Many of you have been involved in this planning.

After that, I'd like to deal with as many questions as you have and listen to any further ideas you might have to make it easier for all of us to realize the benefits with a minimum of disruption.

Offers to make it a dialogue, not a monologue. What follows is the rationale for the decision.

30 Introducing the Ultra 500, a New Strategic Product

Seth Hopkins

In this speech, the speechwriter describes a company called Wide Screen, Inc. The speaker is introducing consumers to its brand new product, a high definition television set on which the company is pegging its future. This is a very aggressive sales pitch and could be used by a company with little recognition and market share but big aspirations. One of the challenges of this speech is that it addresses both internal and external audiences. In other words, in addition to announcing the TV to employees (who already know about it), the speech must also address the questions of distributors, business analysts, and reporters. A speech that does double duty like this is especially difficult to write. The speech's strategy is to sell the product by selling the emotion of what it represents. Notice how the words capture the magic of a new technology, invoke the fear of becoming outdated, and sell the product as both a source of education and entertainment. The speech counters negative stereotypes of television viewing by suggesting that viewers are part of a large and informed global community. It also manages to sell the Ultra Vision 500 without having to dwell on the features of the product, which may be appropriate for an audience of consumers who do not demand a great deal of technical information.

Scoping Document

Event:	Speech introducing strategic product
Theme:	Introducing the Ultra 500
Place:	Anywhere
Date:	Anytime
Audience:	Employees, sales force, industry analysts, distributors, media
Length:	About 9 minutes, 867 words

Speech

When Alexander Graham Bell introduced the telephone, the American public didn't understand what a revolution it would become.

Early investors were skeptical, and leading industrialists of the day publicly asked why anyone would want to make a phone call when telegraph offices existed in nearly every town.

Today, we snicker at the innocence of our ancestors because we understand that Bell's invention didn't just replace the telegraph, but it empowered the world's people in a way that even Bell could not imagine. For a citizen of the 21st century, the world is a very small place—a place where even the most distant relative or business associate can be reached in a matter of seconds just by pressing the right series of buttons on a universal machine that often still bears the name of its inventor.

There is a new invention that's destined to have as great of an impact on American society as the telephone. You may not realize this, but in the next few years, your television will become as obsolete as the telegraph became a century ago. And like the telegraph operators of the time, you probably don't realize that this revolution is on the way.

By 2007, the TV signals that you receive through cable, satellite, or antenna will go silent. . . . America's TV stations will no longer have the right to broadcast on those frequencies, and your equipment will be useless. Every station will be forced to convert to a high definition signal, which means that only the new type of television, HDTV, will work. And unless you own an HDTV or a converter for your old set, all you will see is endless snow. You'll be like the last telegraph operator waiting for someone to listen to.

Talking Points

Setting the context, subtly suggesting that the Ultra 500 is as revolutionary as the telephone.

The speaker's strategy is to create some dramatic tension.

Transition to the actual introduction.

There are people in the audience that need some education.

But that doesn't mean that you won't be able to watch TV. It just means that you will have to buy new equipment to watch it with. Until now, these sets were expensive and cumbersome. I'm pleased to announce that Wide Screen has released an amazing, 53-inch-rear-projection television that will transform your living room into a movie theater.

The actual introduction.

Our Ultra Vision 500 is the lightest and least expensive HDTV in its class, and it comes with everything that you need to assure that your entertainment isn't interrupted when the nation goes digital. *Consumer Reports* recently rated the Ultra Vision 500 "best in class" for remarkable clarity, ease of operation, realistic colors, and precise, sensitive sound.

Note use of inclusive "our."

What does the Ultra Vision offer that your regular TV doesn't? For one thing, you will notice that it's wider than most TVs. High Definition television exists on a 16 by 9 format, which is more like a movie screen than a TV.

Describes the benefits.

But the real surprise comes when you turn it on. Your old set has a few thousand pixels of irregular shaped and crudely covered dots which make up the image. It relies on your brain to trick you into thinking that those basic shapes and colors make sense.

Your new Wide Screen will turn those few thousand dots into over 2 million evenly spaced, intricately colored pixels that give you a moving picture so clear that you'll think a postcard has come to life.

Note use of "your" as if the TV has already been sold.

You may not realize how much time you spend watching television. The average American spends three and a half hours per day being entertained, informed, and educated in front of his most valuable piece of furniture. Nearly half of Americans believe that TV is

Back to the context that creates a business case for the product.

the most authoritative source of information, and three in four say that it is the most influential.

TV isn't just another media in our country, it is a way of life . . . engrained in our culture like no other institution. Since the first sets were unrolled from their crates in the 1930s, our world has forever been transformed. When World War I broke out in 1917, we read about it in the newspapers. But during World War II, we saw, in vivid and horrifying detail, the carnage on the streets of Europe, the goose-stepping Nazis, and the fiery orations of the world's leaders.

Both of these wars had millions of casualties, but ask yourself what you know and remember about each. I'm willing to bet that you know a lot more about World War II. Why? You were able to see and hear it . . . and you're probably conjuring up imagines in your head right now . . . images that you saw thanks to the television industry.

Ask yourself where you were when the World Trade Center was attacked. Did you wait for the newspaper to tell you what happened, or did you immediately turn on the TV? When the United States invaded Iraq, where did you turn for live videos and commentary? In today's society, television has demonstrated that it is as powerful as it's ever been.

Creates sense of immediacy and drama by invoking tragedies and how TV brings America together.

And with the Ultra Vision 500, you can harness this power to its full potential.

Back to the features of the product.

The world is changing. Americans see the world in the vivid reality of HDTV. You are invited to join the revolution. Otherwise, you might find yourself clinging to your old TV with the same passion as the last telegraph operator clung to his past.

Conclusion with a startling image of the costs of getting left behind. Perhaps better would be to start the conclusion with the telegraph operator warning and conclude on a note of looking forward.

Please Join Me in Congratulating Ourselves

John Kador

These are remarks to announce the acquisition of a new major customer, to alert the staff to the customer's special needs, and to get the team on track to make the new relationship a success. The tone of the speech is informal and congratulatory.

Scoping Document

Event:	Company event
Theme:	Announcing new customer
Place:	Anywhere
Date:	Anytime
Audience:	Fellow employees
Length:	About 5 minutes, 552 words

Speech

Good news rarely comes in such an agreeable package.

Please join me in congratulating ourselves for the decision by ABC Corporation, which has just announced to the world the identity of its principal engineering firm.

That firm, thanks to the incredible dedication and teamwork you have all demonstrated, is our firm.

Our firm. Never in the history of our company has that term ever been more true.

It's clear that when ABC Corporation made its decision to go with us, the deciding factor was less the engineering capabilities that we could offer. We all

Talking Points

Preamble to good news.

Now the good news.

Pause for applause.

Emphasis by repetition.

Telling it straight. The firm's value proposition is the teamwork.

know that our competitors have roughly similar capabilities. No, what we offered was a superior level of teamwork and dedication and that combination ABC Corporation could not match anywhere else in the world.

I know that I don't have to tell you what it means to us to have ABC sign with us. It's a huge boost, both financially and to our reputation. All sorts of doors that were closed to us before are suddenly open. We know how good we are. ABC knows how good we are. And because they are such a high-profile client, soon everyone will know how good we are.

This "I know I don't have to tell you . . ." is a paradoxical transition. Of course, the speaker has to tell them. It alerts listeners to something important.

And financially it isn't bad, either. Let me tell you what today's news means to each of us.

Speaker discusses financial specifics.

. . .

Now, of course, we must deliver. And that requires us to execute on the promise of how good we are.

One of our principles is to treat all clients equally. We have built our business one client at a time, and that is how we will continue to build this business. All of our clients are special. All are important.

Review corporate culture.

At the same time, we need to acknowledge that ABC is a very big client, not only in terms of our credibility, but in the immediate billings it represents. ABC will be making huge demands on us, and I want to make you aware of its areas of special concern.

Why this client is special.

Speaker outlines areas of client concern.

. . .

The action plans we develop for this client must reflect these special needs. If that means customizing the features of some of our services, we will not hesitate to do so. We want to take a very responsive approach to this client.

While few of us will not have direct or indirect engagement with the emerging ABC projects, all of us have a responsibility to making sure we all meet our deliverables.

Use the speech to spur increased commitment.

We want to have one point of contact with the ABC account. That is important as we want to be able to speak with one voice.

Be specific about the requirements.

Let me introduce the project management team primarily responsible for the ABC account.
They are:

Speaker introduces client account team by name.

. . .

Please direct all communications concerning ABC to Jack Smith. In particular, any questions regarding billing, scheduling, or performance issues need to go through Bill Wilson.

The speech becomes more personal with these names, and it also gives a boost to the individuals named.

So congratulations again. But now we have the hard work to do. We represented ourselves as the very best, and we are. Now ABC expects us to demonstrate our excellence. I know that we will have no difficulty doing so. We are the best.

Moves beyond self-congratulations.

It's great to have ABC's validation of our excellence on the scoreboard.

Transition to closing.

But as my old basketball coach used to say, you can't play the game if you're watching the scoreboard.

Sports metaphor recalls teamwork analogy.

It's time to get our eyes on the work ahead of us.
Let's get going.

PART 4

Ceremonial Speeches and Remarks

CHAPTER 8

Speeches for Tributes, Anniversaries, Dedications, and Welcoming Remarks

TRIBUTES

Tribute speeches honor or celebrate a person, a group, an institution, or an event. They differ from award or congratulatory speeches in their formality. For that reason, tribute speeches are out of favor in the business world. When occasion calls for a tribute speech, it is more often than not to honor an entire group or class of people such as teachers, soldiers, or mothers. For example, on Memorial Day the leader of a veterans' organization might deliver a speech of tribute to commemorate soldiers who died defending the interests of the United States. For a business example, consider a ground-breaking ceremony for the construction of a new factory. Here the governor of the state may give a speech honoring the company for creating thousands of jobs.

Inspiration and tribute go together. The fundamental purpose of a speech of tribute is not merely to inform your audience, but to inspire them. The speaker should stimulate and heighten audience members' adoration for the person, group, institution, or event being honored. In preparing a tribute speech, here are six guidelines to keep in mind. The speech of tribute should be

- Generous with praise.
- Thoroughly positive.
- Specific—The remarks should be so specific that they could not be said about anyone else or for any other occasion.

- Personal—Make your speech of tribute reveal a real human being who is personable and vulnerable.
- Inspirational—The remarks should stir sentiments, causing people to feel joy, hope, or excitement. The speaker should attempt to uplift the audience.
- Sincere.

32 Tribute to James R. Houghton: One of America's Great CEOs

Roger G. Ackerman, Corning

Roger G. Ackerman is former chairman of Corning Incorporated. His remarks were in tribute to James R. Houghton, whom he replaced as chairman and CEO in 1996, upon Houghton's retirement. In April 2002, Mr. Houghton returned as chairman and CEO. Houghton joined Corning in 1962, serving in the areas of production, finance, and sales over the next three years. In 1969, he was elected a director of the company; in 1971 he became vice chairman with responsibility for Corning's international operations; and in 1983, he advanced to chairman and CEO. Mr. Houghton remained a member of the company's board of directors, with his original retirement as chairman in 1996. One of the indispensable duties of a new CEO or chairman is to pay eloquent tribute to the person he or she replaces. The job is made easier when, as in this case, the successor has genuine respect and affection for the incumbent.

Scoping Document

Event:	1995 annual shareholders meeting
Theme:	Tribute to former chairman and CEO
Place:	Corning headquarters, Corning, New York
Date:	April 25, 1996
Audience:	Approximately 5,000 Corning investors
Length:	About 10 minutes, 1,061 words

Speech

It has been said of great men that they bring out greatness in others. That by their vision, they turn weakness into strength, obstacles into opportunities, and challenges into triumphs. And in the end, they leave behind in others, a conviction and a passion for success.

Talking Points

Impassioned introduction signals that this is a tribute speech.

Such a man—and so much more—is James R. Houghton. He's given Corning 34 years of distinguished service—for the last 13 as our leader. And in my opinion, he's one of the greatest CEOs this country has ever produced.

Introduces incumbent. By convention the speaker starts with a formal reference (note middle initial), and then moves to more informal terms.

He is a leader in the most enlightened sense—a visionary, a thinker, a man of action, a change-maker, a friend, a teacher, and a man of infinite integrity and compassion. His deeds bear this out.

As chairman and CEO, he took a 130-year-old company with a grand history and set it on a course for a glorious future. He made Corning a modern, high-tech, global company and prepared us for the rich opportunities of the 21st century. And he did it at a time in history when hostile corporate takeovers and a swift rise in global competition were shaking the business world to its roots.

Describes career. Note statements all start with "He" in rule of three.

During Jamie's tenure as chairman and CEO, roughly half of the companies listed on the *Fortune* 500 fell by the wayside. But Corning didn't. Since Jamie took over as chairman in 1983, company sales have grown from $1.5 billion to $5.3 billion.

Suddenly it's "Jamie."

What's striking about this record is how it was attained. Building on the strengths of the past, Jamie redefined the way we do business and led us into the global, high-tech, marketplace of The Information Age. He gave us a focal point, a direction, and he called it Total Quality Management.

It was a courageous move to implement so broad a cultural change in 1983 when the company was seriously struggling. But—as Jamie taught us time and time again—growth demands change. And grow we did. Total Quality improved all of our operations.

It drove our strategy and took us to leadership positions in the dynamic, growth fields of communications, the environment, and health care . . . as defined by Fortune magazine. . . .

Talks at some length about total quality management (omitted).

Now, I can go on and on about Corning's performance under Jamie's leadership. His record of achievement is clear. But what's more important, what's more rare, is an intangible quality of leadership that he possesses, which you won't find on any balance sheet. For lack of a better name, let's call it his "Leadership Spirit."

Uses vocabulary of business ("intangible" assets) to describe Houghton.

Jamie's first priority was the individual. He really cares about people and the culture they work in. He consistently looked for ways to improve the work environment to help people do their jobs better. That's why he's so often stressed our corporate values.

Corning's values are the unchanging, moral and ethical compass for this organization, and guide us every day. We can be thankful that Jamie instilled in us their importance and their permanence.

How correct his vision was. Today, easy access to technology is leveling the playing field among business rivals. Going forward, what will provide the edge and make a company stand out from the competition will be the skills and spirit of its people. Jamie knew that a winning organization needed a climate where people could contribute and grow.

Makes the case that ethics and values offer competitive advantage.

Jamie epitomized a key quality of leadership. He led by example. He walked the talk. He also understood that personal success comes from group success. So he was a team player, and he shared decision-making responsibilities broadly with his team. Jamie was quick to accept blame when things went wrong.

List of attributes.

However, he was even quicker to lavish praise on others when things went right. He was courageous. He was a risk-taker. He was unafraid to break with convention. He remained—ever—open, flexible, and willing to entertain new ideas.

Above all, he understood that leadership is a responsibility, not a privilege. Therefore, he always put the interests of people and the company above himself. He nurtured and developed strong subordinates, thereby paving the way for his last lesson on the "art of change"— his succession.

In some of his speeches—and Jamie, forgive me for borrowing this—he used a story to make a point about how leadership must yield to change. It involved an exam being given to flight cadets in the Australian Air Force.

If the honoree is in the room, it is a good idea to address him or her personally.

One question asked of the cadets was: what would they do if the Prime Minister fell out of a plane that they were flying. There were some very creative answers, from swooping down to catch the Prime Minister, to disappearing into the Outback and going AWOL. The correct answer? Adjust flaps to compensate for the weight change.

Humorous anecdote.

Jamie's point was that if American industry was to reclaim a leadership position, workers must become "pilots"—flying their planes without reliance on the higher ups.

So Jamie, we're adjusting our flaps. But, succeeding you is not easy. You are either a living legend or an icon—I'm not sure what. But I know that I'm not an icon.

Speaks to honoree indirectly.

Well, we're not going to replace Jamie Houghton. How can you replace this extraordinary man? We're going to carry on his tradition of success—a tradition that now resides fiercely in those of us who follow him.

Another convention of tribute speeches is to acknowledge that it is quite impossible to replace the honoree.

We're going to hold to and build on Corning's corporate values, like he did. We're going to continue to advance the skills and knowledge of our people and unleash their creativity, like he did because they are this company's most important asset. We're going to anticipate change in the marketplace, and make changes ourselves, as we need to, like he did. We're going to grow this company from the strong and healthy roots that you—Jamie—have cultivated.

Transition to end signaled by bold statement and persistent use of sentences starting with "we're."

As we turn this page in our history, we may feel a little frightened, a little uncertain. But we do well to remember that it was you Jamie who taught us how—and encouraged us—to embrace change. Our feelings today reflect some very mixed emotions. On the one hand, sadness old friend. On the other excitement about the great opportunities before us.

I want to close with a simple thank you, Jamie, from the bottom of our hearts—for your spirit; for your vision; for your strength and for your integrity; and for the passion for growth and success that you have instilled in all of us.

Ends with personal thanks to the honoree. And ends with an important word, "us."

33

Beginning of a New Millennium

Robert Yahng, American Bridge Company

In this speech at the dedication of its new corporate headquarters, Chairman of the Board Robert Yahng offers a look at American Bridge Company in an historical context, both global and personal. American Bridge Company was organized on April 14, 1900, by J.P. Morgan and Co. as a consolidation of 27 major bridge fabricating and construction companies. It became the premier steel contractor in the world, building such major bridges as the San Francisco–Oakland Bay Bridge, the Mackinac Straits Bridge in Michigan, and the Verrazano Narrows Bridge in New York. Mr. Yahng is based in San Francisco.

Scoping Document

Event:	Company meeting
Theme:	Dedication of new corporate headquarters
Place:	Company headquarters, Coraopolis, Pennsylvania
Date:	June 2000
Audience:	Employees and their families
Length:	About 3 minutes, 344 words

Speech

As most of you are aware, this year marks the 100-year anniversary of the founding of our company.

We don't have available a list of all the companies started that year, but my guess is that very few of them remain today, and certainly none performed so well over the entire breadth of the 20th Century.

From the Hell Gate Bridge at the beginning of the last century to the Lions Gate at the beginning of

Talking Points

Gets right to the point.

Dramatizes the point that 100 years in the life of a company is a huge accomplishment.

Specific projects support the main point: The company

this one, no company has constructed more landmarks or one-of-a-kind structures around the world than American Bridge.

is something to be proud of.

What truly makes us unique is that we are as poised today to repeat our success in the 21st Century as we were when we were first incorporated 100 years ago.

Promise and expectation to keep up the accomplishment.

For most of our history, we were the preeminent steel fabricator and erector in the world. Over 14 fabrication facilities, coupled with our unparalleled construction capability, enabled us to win almost any job we went after.

A company used to occupying a leadership position.

However, major changes in the steel industry in the 1970s and 1980s resulted in the elimination of this fabricating capability and the narrowing of our market to large steel erection projects in the United States. Over the past six years, we have redefined ourselves and are now structured as a general contractor/design builder with a manufacturing capability. We have a new strategic plan, which defines our goals, our strategy to meet those goals, and our structure to meet that strategy.

Establishes some historical context for business challenges.

Reasons why the company will meet the challenges.

Over the course of my career, I can recall one constant when I think of American Bridge.

At any time across the country, we have always had the best people in the industry. When you consider all the projects over all the years, it is amazing that our reputation has remained so strong for so long. The reason for this is, of course, our people.

Sharing the credit.

Giving credit to the people.

You cannot sustain the best name in the business without the best people in the business. This remains true today and is the primary reason why I am so confident of our future.

The bottom line. The people that made the past so successful will continue to do so in the future.

The best is yet to be.

End with hopeful promise.

34

100 Years of Jell-O: Still the Coolest

Todd Brown, Kraft Foods

A senior executive of Kraft Foods, Inc. delivered these remarks at the Jell-O 100th Anniversary Party in New York City on April 8, 1997. It's always a plus to be able to speak about something as familiar to people as Jell-O, and it's even more of a plus to be able to have Bill Cosby assist you. Watch how the speaker leverages the audience's total identification with Jell-O.

Scoping Document

Event:	Product anniversary party
Theme:	100th birthday of Jell-O
Place:	New York, New York
Date:	April 8, 1997
Audience:	Approximately 5,000 industry dignitaries, Kraft employees, media
Length:	About 13 minutes, 1,312 words

Speech

Good evening and welcome to the 100th anniversary party for Jell-O . . . a true American cultural institution.

I am talking major institution here, folks... as in "the Stars and Stripes" and "apple pie" . . . and "backyard barbecues on the Fourth of July." I'm talking as American as The Statue of Liberty and The World Series and The Smithsonian . . . as American as family reunions at Thanksgiving . . . as American as Mark Twain, Will Rogers and The Three Stooges . . . as American as rhythm and blues, rock 'n' roll . . . and jazz.

Talking Points

Comes straight to the point — why they are there.

Dramatizes the subject by setting up Jell-O with other icons of America.

Jell-O is the largest-selling prepared dessert in America. Thirteen boxes of Jell-O brand gelatin are sold every second—that's over six hundred boxes just since I started talking.

Business context of product.

And on an average day, more than 1.1 million boxes of Jell-O are purchased or eaten. That is a heck of a lot of Jell-O. In fact, if the boxes representing one year's production were laid end to end, they'd reach three-fifths of the way around the world—from New York to China!

Violates the rule about loading up a phrase with statistics, but here it works because the visual is so memorable.

Jell-O is everywhere, not just on our tables. Over the years, it's made frequent appearances in American popular art and film. It's played a cameo role in such Hollywood movies as *Some Like It Hot* . . . *Jurassic Park* . . . *Kindergarten Cop* . . . and, most recently, *Ghosts of Mississippi.*

Employees are not just making gelatin, but making a vital part of America.

All of which gives you a peek at the mystique of Jell-O. It has its own essence, yet it can be almost anything we want. It's never the center of attention, but you always know it's there.

Did you know Jell-O had a mystique?

Clearly Jell-O resonates with all of us, and in some very interesting ways. In fact—and I'm not making this up—a doctor in Canada once hooked Jell-O up to an EEG machine . . . and found that its movement is virtually identical to the brain waves of a healthy adult man or woman!

I hope he's making this up!

As our society and culture have gone through one era after another, Jell-O has reinvented itself to fit with Americans' needs and lifestyles. So it's no wonder that the Jell-O trademark is recognized by 99 percent of all Americans . . . or that Jell-O is found in almost two-thirds of the nation's kitchens. (And frankly, I think the other one-third has at least *one* box, hidden

Jell-O is one of the world's most recognized brands.

somewhere in the back of the cupboard, behind the
Shake 'n' Bake.)

But really, you don't need me to tell you about our
long-running love affair with Jell-O. The truth is
there in your own lives . . . right there in the Jell-O
memories that you've shared with us and that are
posted on the walls here.

Evoking Jell-O memories draws audience into speech.

Some of you recalled favorite dishes . . . like "when
father would crush it up and add milk and sugar.
Yum!" . . . or "my Grandmother's Jell-O/pecan/fruit
salad; she makes it every Thanksgiving" . . . or
"orange Jell-O with little teeny Mandarin oranges."

Jell-O figures into many family stories.

Others recalled Jell-O experiences: "listening to Jack
Benny sing 'J-E-L-L- O'" . . . or "Mom giving me red
Jell-O when I had the flu" . . . or "the way my father
makes Jell-O and acts as if he has just prepared a
gourmet six-course meal."

No question about it, Jell-O has a rich and colorful
history . . . and it's been a presence in so many of our
lives. I said earlier that Jell-O is an authentic cultural
icon, and it's not hard to see why: year after year,
decade after decade, like every great and enduring
brand, it's stayed fresh, contemporary, and relevant.

Restating main theme.

We want to make sure that the next 100 years of
Jell-O will be just as full of fun, good eating, and
fond memories. So let's talk about today—and
tomorrow.

Promise to extend the accomplishments of the past into the future.

Among the newest items in the Jell-O family . . . is a
Sparkling White Grape Flavor: The Champagne of
Jell-O," which we're unveiling tonight. We'll be
introducing it this year—as a special edition—available for a limited time only.

Jell-O is not a static product. There are always innovations.

That's the great thing about Jell-O: it can be almost anything; it can fit in almost anywhere. Champagne Jell-O? Hey, why not? *Food and Wine* magazine agrees: it's already published its list of the hottest foods for 1997, and the editors named our new Jell-O product a hot trend for this year.

As we keep up with Americans' palates and lifestyles, we're also staying up-to-the-minute in the ways we communicate with everyone who loves Jell-O. Jell-O fans who log onto the Kraft website—at kraftfoods.com—will find a special area devoted to Jell-O.

Jell-O on the Internet.

But wait—there's more. Tonight I'm pleased to announce two exciting, fun projects—one that will celebrate the colorful history of Jell-O . . . and another devoted to its future.

The "But wait . . ." indicates a transition point in the speech.

The historical project is a Jell-O museum in LeRoy, New York.

The folks in LeRoy take great pride in the fact that their town is the home of the man who invented the modern version of Jell-O and of his wife, who gave the product its name.

Speech is now organized to talk about the past and the future.

The people of LeRoy already have a lot of Jell-O memorabilia . . . and they'll be doing some really creative things to celebrate this anniversary along with us.

In July, they'll hold a Jell-O Jubilee. And when the museum opens, there'll be a "Jell-O Brick Road." It's a pathway that leads to the museum. It's financed by private donations, and there's a sizable stretch of bricks underwritten by Kraft Foods and dedicated to Bill Cosby.

Bill Cosby is the long-standing celebrity spokesman for Jell-O.

The other project I want to announce tonight . . . is one that looks forward to the exciting future of Jell-O. This year—and for the two years after that—Jell-O is going to appear in yet another characteristically American venue: the Macy's Thanksgiving Day Parade.

Transition to tomorrow.

The Parade is now in its 70th year. It's a showcase for the country's top marching bands, plus celebrities, plus unique performing ensembles. It will be seen by two million people along the parade route . . . and millions more watching on TV. Its atmosphere of color, excitement, and family fun are almost as American as Thanksgiving itself.

Review of another American institution, the Thanksgiving Day Parade, for context.

And this year, Jell-O is going to be a part of all that. Along with all the clowns, marching bands, giant balloons, and Santa Claus himself the 1997 Parade will include a float devoted to Jell-O.

Jell-O and the Macy's Parade.

Like the Parade itself, our float will be colorful, exciting, and fun. And like Jell-O itself, the float will move and wiggle. How is that going to work? Tune in to NBC on Thanksgiving morning and find out!

Similarities between Jell-O and the parade.

So there you have a look back at the history of Jell-O . . . and a look forward at its future.

Summary of past and future.

All of our Jell-O people, I assure you, are looking forward. We're working very hard to make sure that the next 100 years will be just as terrific as the last . . . and that many years from now, not only your kids, but their kids too . . . will smile when they recall their very own "Jell-O memories" . . . and they will agree, one and all, that Jell-O is "still the coolest."

But the emphasis is on the future.

Multigenerational appeal.

In a few minutes, we'll have the special treat you've all been waiting for—a special, no-cover, no-mini-

Announcing presentation by Bill Cosby!

mum performance just for us, by the incomparable Bill Cosby. But first, we're going to take you on a little video journey . . . through the history of Jell-O. It's a celebration of the Jell-O memories that we all share, with music, commercials, trivia, and a lot of other fun stuff.

[Plays video of Cosby performance.]

Thank you, Bill . . . that was wonderful! Just terrific! We really do appreciate your being here and taking part in our celebration.

All of us at Jell-O . . . are extremely grateful to Bill. His comic genius and the very special rapport he has with kids . . . have made powerful contributions to the success of Jell-O . . . for nearly a quarter of its 100-year history.

Gratitude to Bill Cosby for being associated with Jell-O.

And I'd like to thank you all for coming.

Appreciates the audience.

But the party's not over. In fact, it's just beginning. I hope you brought your appetites, because we have our new products for you to sample—Champagne Jell-O, the new No-Bake dessert, and the rest.

As the speaker ends, he creates more excitement for upcoming activities.

So eat, party, and have a great time!

35 Raytheon at 80

Daniel P. Burnham, Raytheon

These brief remarks were delivered on the occasion of the 80th anniversary of the founding of Raytheon Company. Chief Executive Officer Daniel P. Burnham spoke these words at an 80th Anniversary event at Raytheon Company's headquarters in Lexington, Massachusetts, July 11, 2002.

Scoping Document

Event:	Company meeting
Theme:	80th Anniversary Celebration
Place:	Company headquarters, Lexington, Massachusetts
Date:	July 11, 2002
Audience:	Approximately 2,000 employees and their families
Length:	About 2 minutes, 281 words

Speech

Thank you for coming! Welcome to all who are participating by Web-cast across the United States and around the world. Thank you for joining in this celebration of your accomplishments.

As you just saw, on Monday, I had the opportunity to close the day of trading on the New York Stock Exchange, with this gavel, to celebrate our 80th anniversary in business, and 50 years listed on the exchange.

It was an exhilarating moment that was extremely well coordinated, thanks to many people including your colleagues in this building, especially Amy Hosmer and Tim Oliver.

Talking Points

[Just played a videotape.]

Displays the gavel as a prop.

It was very appropriate. After all, there aren't too many companies that can say they're 80 years old!

Probably better to talk in terms of "we" than "they."

During those 80 years, the United States and its allies have experienced booms and busts, a World War, a Cold War and a Desert Storm. But always, always, we've enjoyed Enduring Freedom.

Repetition as emphasis.

And always, the people of Raytheon have been developing and producing systems and providing services, that have helped protect our freedoms and improve our quality of life.

Rule of three.

That includes our employees throughout the U.S. and around the world, including our colleagues at Raytheon Systems Limited in the UK. RSL coincidentally is celebrating several milestones:

The 50th anniversary of the introduction of secondary radar at the Harlow site.

The centenary of the manufacture of the first cathode ray tube in Britain, accomplished by RSL's predecessor UK company, Cossor.

And 40 years in aircraft servicing at the Broughton site.

Abrupt ending. A more forward-looking conclusion would be better.

36

The Best Is Yet to Be: Celebrating the 100th Anniversary of American Bridge Company

Robert H. Luffy, American Bridge Company

In this speech at the dedication of the new corporate headquarters, Robert H. Luffy, president and CEO, offers a look at American Bridge Company in an historical context, both global and personal. American Bridge Company was organized on April 14, 1900, by J.P. Morgan and Co. as a consolidation of 27 major bridge fabricating and construction companies. It became the premier steel contractor in the world, building such major bridges as the San Francisco–Oakland Bay Bridge, the Mackinac Straits Bridge in Michigan, and the Verrazano Narrows Bridge in New York. Mr. Luffy, based in Pittsburgh, assumed his present position in 1993.

Scoping Document

Event:	Company meeting
Theme:	Dedication of new corporate headquarters
Place:	Company headquarters, Coraopolis, Pennsylvania
Date:	June 2000
Audience:	Employees and their families
Length:	About 4 minutes, 369 words

Speech

This afternoon, I wish to share with you a few personal thoughts that came into my mind when I think of this grand new building.

I think of American Bridge in historical context, both global and personal.

Talking Points

The speech immediately becomes personal. "Grand new building' is a nice phrase.

Suggests a two-part structure to the speech.

In 1865, the Civil War ended.

Even though he doesn't announce it, the speech starts with the historical.

In 1868, my great grandfather came to this country from China.

In 1870, American Bridge was formed in Chicago to build wood and iron bridges.

Such a laundry list recitation of dates bored us in history class, but here it seems to work.

In 1900, J.P. Morgan merged American Bridge with 27 other erection and fabrication companies and began the American Bridge we know today.

Notice how the chronological statements start simple and get longer and more personal.

In 1935, Japan invaded China, and in the World War that followed, Japan slaughtered many more civilians in China than all the lives lost in the Holocaust. They devastated China. As part of its war campaign, Japan began the systematic bombing of bridges there.

It was then that America came to China's aid, and American Bridge traveled to China and began to rebuild the bridges that the Japanese destroyed.

Foreshadows patriotic conclusion.

In those years, my father-in-law, Glyn Ing, was a young engineer, and as he fled from the Japanese advances, the presence of American Bridge made a lasting impression on him.

Brings in the family connection.

Thus when the opportunity arose in the 1980s to invest in American Bridge, he seized it. He did so not with greed and profit foremost in his mind, but with deeply felt appreciation.

Coming from the San Francisco Bay area, I can tell you what business executives in Silicon Valley say about the components of success.

Transition to the second part of the speech.

They tell me that if you have a quality product and good market demand for that product, those elements are not enough to create success. They state that 20 percent of a company's success can be attributed to the quality product; 20 percent to the strong market demand.

But 60 percent of a company's success is directly attributable to the management and personnel of a company. That includes all of you, especially people like Betty Back who is completing her 43rd year in the Company.

Acknowledges and individual by name.

This year marks the end of the 20th Century, and the beginning of a new millennium.

Set of parallel statements.

This year marks the end of American Bridge's 1st Century, and the beginning of our new millennium. May God Bless America, and may God Bless American Bridge.

Patriotic ending.

37

Messages from the Heart: An R.R. Donnelley Celebration in Brazil

Joseph C. Lawler, R.R. Donnelley

Joseph Lawler, executive vice president of R.R. Donnelley delivered these remarks to dedicate the grand opening of its new consolidated book facility in Brazil on July 31, 2002. Notice that the speaker spends no time at all describing the facility itself. The speech is all about relationships, the commitment of the parent company, and the shared love of books.

Scoping Document

Event:	Company meeting
Theme:	Dedication of facility in Brazil
Place:	Tamboré, Brazil
Date:	July 31, 2002
Audience:	Customers, employees and their families
Length:	About 9 minutes, 942 words

Speech

To our great customers . . . our honored guests . . . and our esteemed R.R. Donnelley employees here in Tamboré . . . I would like to say:

Boa noite (Good evening) . . . and thank you for being here today.

I also want to say how excited I am to be here . . . and how happy I am to have the opportunity to return to Brazil.

I love visiting this country.

Talking Points

Starts remarks in a formal way.

When in a foreign country, it's good to say a few words in the local language (Portuguese in Brazil).

Your winters are mild . . .

Your music is inspiring . . .

Your coffee is outstanding . . .

Series of short statements sets up a rhythm, almost poetic.

And, of course, your soccer team is the best in the world.

Three short statements culminating with an "and" statement.

But most of all, I love visiting here because of the people.

Brazilians are some of the kindest . . . friendliest . . . and most sincere people I have ever met. And your energy and enthusiasm for your work is an example to everyone around the world.

This speech is a poem to the people of Brazil.

One of the things I like best about the people here is your ability to speak from the heart. I am reminded of a proverb I heard quoted in Portuguese, which says:

A boca expressa o que caracão sente.

Proverb. (The mouth speaks what the heart feels.)

Today, I would like to share with you three messages straight from my heart as to why I'm feeling full of excitement for what we are doing here in Brazil.

Promises three messages.

My first message is that I am extremely proud of our Tamboré facility.

First message.

It is the largest and most modern book production site in the region—representing a true milestone in book printing here in Brazil and in Latin America . . .

It joins together two tremendous and talented groups of people from separate R.R. Donnelley operations under one roof—employing 500 people in the printing and binding of books, and 200 more in areas such as maintenance, cafeteria and security staff . . .

And it features an optimized layout and workflow— allowing us to serve our customers more efficiently and cost effectively . . . and from one location instead of two.

I am also proud of what this facility stands for.

It stands for the readers of Brazil, who are increasing in number and in their thirst for quality and variety in what they read.

Connecting statements with a common introductory phrase ("It stands . . .").

It stands for our good friends, the book publishers of Brazil, who are providing the quality and variety that readers are asking for.

It stands for the largest buyer of books in the world— the Brazilian government.

It stands for education, which accounts for 60 percent of all the books sold in Brazil.

And it stands for a future in which anyone, anywhere, can read a book and create a better life.

Here is my second message:

Second message.

I am extremely passionate about R.R. Donnelley's vision and how this facility enables our vision to come alive in Latin America.

Our vision is all about people. Specifically, it says that R.R. Donnelley will, "enrich lives by connecting people with the power of words and images."

Books do enrich lives. They do help people connect with each other. They inform. They educate. They entertain. They do bring us together.

We are proud, at R.R. Donnelley, to be part of the book business. And we are proud to be part of YOUR book business, here in Brazil.

Being part of your book business, however, requires us to do business differently today than we did in the past. In today's business world, our customers need far more than print and bind.

That is why—in support of our vision—R.R. Donnelley's strategy is to become a communications solutions provider . . . a single source of communications effectiveness.

We define communications effectiveness as:

"Moving focused content . . . to select consumers . . . with the least waste . . . lowest total cost . . . and greatest results."

In other words, our strategy requires us to eliminate waste, eliminate cost and start a flow of information and knowledge that enables book publishers to succeed in completely new ways.

As the world's leading provider of communications services, we will be much more than an excellent printer. We are already doing that today with several of our customers here in Brazil.

That is what it means to be a communications services provider.

That is what it means to focus not just on communications efficiency—but on communications *effectiveness*.

And that brings me to my third message: I am excited about the business opportunities here in Latin America and the growth potential I see in the future.

Third message.

What we are doing here is an essential part of R.R. Donnelley's International operations, and our International operations are an essential part of our corporate strategy . . . an essential part of our brand . . . an essential part of who we are as a company.

Our commitment to this facility is a long-term investment in this region . . . to work with some of the finest publishers in the world who are creating important work that needs to be communicated in efficient ways.

We are working hard to grow with you in the years to come.

We intend to grow throughout Brazil . . . throughout Latin America . . . and throughout Europe and Asia.

We intend to be the world's leading provider of communications services.

And you—our customers, our employees, and our government leaders—you will help us get there.

To that end, my final message—straight from the heart—is simply: *muito obrigado*. (Thank you very much.)

Transition to closing with another bit of Portuguese.

Thank you to our employees . . . for your dedication, your enthusiasm and your commitment to living R.R. Donnelley's vision and values here in Brazil . . .

Statements all beginning with the same phrase set up a memorable rhythm to the closing.

Thank you to our customers . . . for making the
Latin American book market what it is today
through your excellent publications and through
your understanding of what your customers want . . .

Thank you to the government and community
leaders . . . for supporting business, education and
literacy in Brazil and throughout Latin America . . .

And, most of all, thank you to the Brazilian and
Latin American people . . . for loving books as much
as we do at R.R. Donnelley.

*Conclusion that ends with an
image of books seems right.*

Welcome to WasteTech—2001

John Kador

An example of a speech welcoming delegates to a conference. This conference happens to be on waste management, but the format would be similar to any professional or industrial conference.

Scoping Document

Event:	WasteTech—2001 conference
Theme:	Waste management
Place:	Dallas, Texas
Date:	Anytime
Audience:	Conference attendees
Length:	About 2 minutes, 195 words

Speech

It gives me a great pleasure to invite you to Dallas to take part in this unprecedented event on waste management.

Over the last decades of the 20th century waste management and recycling have emerged as a very serious and difficult to solve problem of both economic and socio-political importance.

That's why putting into practice correct waste management policy has become a vital necessity for countries all over the world. As a result it could serve not only for environment protection but also for efficient economical development and social stability.

Talking Points

Welcome.

Puts the business of the conference in broader context.

The success of the first conference, with the support of the International Solid Waste Association, ensured us of the importance and necessity of such waste management forum. The decision of holding this conference in 2001 was strongly supported by federal and local authorities as well as representatives of scientific, industrial and public communities.

Reminds attendees that this work is a continuation of last year's conference.

With over 500 Congress participants and about 100 companies—exhibitors from Russia, the CIS and abroad, WasteTech—2001 is expected to become the international meeting place for waste sector professionals.

I am sure that your participation in WasteTech—2001 will be fruitful and look forward for our meeting in Baltimore in May 2002.

Looking ahead.

CHAPTER 9

Speeches for Presenting and Accepting Awards

For every award, there is a presentation speech and for every presentation speech there is an equal and opposite acceptance speech.

PRESENTATIONS

Whenever an individual is honored, whether or not an actual gift or award is bestowed, a presentation speech is part of the package. The basic premise of a presentation speech is to honor the person to whom the award is being presented and to acknowledge the recipient's achievements. The goal of the presentation speech is to express the organization's gratitude, usually to an individual but sometimes to a group, and usually by the presentation of a physical token of that gratitude. The presentation speech should identify the individual or organization making the presentation, the nature of the contributed gift or award, and the purpose for its being given. In presenting an award speech, keep three things in mind: the honoree to receive the award, the organization on whose behalf the award is presented, and the nature of the occasion.

Speeches and remarks of congratulations honor an individual with appreciation for some tangible accomplishment such as the award of a patent, the publication of a book, a promotion, an anniversary, or other good work. It is unnecessary to address everything the award recipient has ever accomplished in his or her life; rather, focus on achievements and contributions relevant to the award, and address these accomplishments in a manner that will make them relevant to the audience as well as the special occasion. Presentation speeches should:

- Keep opening comments brief
- Present, in chronological order, the achievements of the award recipient and the reasons for presenting the award to this individual
- Present the gift.

39 | The Best Is Yet to Be: Too Busy to Grow Old

Roger B. Smith, General Motors

Roger B. Smith is a retired chairman of General Motors Corporation. His remarks were presented at the Gift Presentation of the longest-tenured GM employee in Sandusky, Ohio. GM asked that the name of the individual not be used, so for the purposes of this speech, we'll call him Mark Smith.

Scoping Document

Event:	Company meeting
Theme:	Retirement award
Place:	Sandusky, Ohio
Date:	May 6, 1988
Audience:	Employees
Length:	About 2 minutes, 266 words

Speech	Talking Points
Someone once said that "growing old is a habit that a busy man has no time to form." That's certainly true of Mark Smith.	*Provocative quote to start.*
	Immediately introduces the subject of the speech.
Mark, you and your long GM career . . . your many contributions to our company . . . your seemingly limitless energy—all of that tells that you really have been too busy to grow old.	*Switches to first name basis.*
But there's something else going on here, too. I just read about some psychological research that shows that specific forms of human intelligence actually	*Waxing eloquent about growing older.*

increase during the middle and later years of life. It turns out that the ability to use an accumulated body of knowledge—known as "crystallized intelligence"—for decision making and problem solving really does improve over a lifetime.

Those findings, of course, have tremendous implications; they tell us that older employees can indeed learn new job skills . . . can indeed be productive throughout their careers.

Asserts the value of older employees.

To me, that's a point worth emphasizing. In our culture, which does so much to idealize youth, it's appropriate, every now and then, to push the pendulum in the other direction.

Acknowledges that we live in a youth-oriented culture.

Mark, I think all of this applies to you. Over the years, you've become more valuable to GM.

Every speech has a topic sentence. For this speech, this is it.

That's why it's such a pleasure to present you with this clock which I hope will be a worthy addition to your collection. Now that I think of it, there's probably no more fitting hobby for a man who has been such good friends with Father Time.

Presents award.

Congratulations, Mark, and thanks. We're grateful for all that you've done for GM, and you have our warmest wishes for years and years of happiness and health.

Thanks the employee on behalf of GM so it's fitting to use "we."

40

Heartiest Congratulations to the Community Chest

Dr. Yaacob Ibrahim, Ministry of Community Development and Sports

Dr. Yaacob Ibrahim, acting minister for the Ministry of Community Development and Sports, Singapore, gave this speech at the 18th annual Community Chest Awards presentation ceremony in Singapore. His congratulatory remarks focused on thanking everyone profusely and trotting out examples of the good work being done by the volunteers. On occasions like this, speakers are well advised to stick to the good news and emphasize the accomplishments. Everyone wants to feel they have accomplished something. The challenges are best left for another day.

Scoping Document

Event:	The 18th Community Chest Awards Presentation Ceremony
Theme:	Awards presentation
Place:	Singapore
Date:	October 18, 2002
Audience:	Employees, guests, local activists, dignitaries
Length:	About 5 minutes, 544 words

Speech

We are here today to show our appreciation to the many organizations that have touched the lives of the needy in our community.

Although these are not the best of times for our economy, you have nevertheless continued to generously help those who may be left behind. In fact, it is in times like these that the disabled, the sick, the elderly or families in distress, have a greater need for our

Talking Points

Gets right to the point, using the inclusive "we."

community's care and compassion to keep their hopes up in working towards a better future.

Community involvement on the part of corporations and organizations is not about giving handouts. It is about giving skills, confidence and hope to the less fortunate so that they can lead more meaningful, independent lives.

Elaborates on the meaning of corporate social responsibility.

Through the Community Chest, you have helped to empower and enable the less fortunate, by providing much needed resources for the many voluntary welfare organization programs and services funded by ComChest. These community-based programs and services equip the less fortunate with the necessary life-skills and strengths to cope with the demands of life.

It is a great credit to Singaporeans—individuals, companies, schools and other organizations alike— that while they may have had to tighten their belts in recent years, they have in fact given even more generously to the community.

Praise for the people of Singapore.

While I am happy with the steady increase in the charity dollar which is timely and needed, what is even more heartening is the indication this gives about the health of our society. It shows that more of us recognize that giving back to society is part of our social responsibility. It is also a sign of strong community bonding among Singaporeans.

Continues to praise the efforts of the community.

We have seen a significant increase in the number of corporate award recipients for this year's Community Chest Awards. While there were only 30 corporate award recipients in the previous year, this has more than doubled to 65 corporate award recipients this year.

Offer encouraging statistics whenever possible.

This can be attributed to the growing endorsement of corporate citizenship in Singapore. Many of the award recipients here today already have an established corporate philosophy of community involvement at their work place.

Corporations are a catalyst that multiplies the small but significant contributions of individual employees. For example, when the SHARE committee under the Community Chest began the "Just One" Campaign, it encouraged the Housing and Development Board staff to contribute just one more dollar every month to the SHARE program.

Other organizations that have been a pillar of strength to the Community Chest, through their sustained and continued support over the years are, namely the Singapore Armed Forces and the Singapore Police Force. I would like to take this opportunity to thank them for their generous contributions and unflagging support of the less fortunate in our society all these years.

Thanks other agencies.

The corporations and organizations that I have highlighted all have one thing in common—they do not merely pay lip service to community service. They practice what they preach, and in so doing, demonstrate that the true essence of corporate citizenship lies in providing for the good of the community. These organizations are worthy standard bearers and I hope that many more will join their ranks.

What do they have in common?

On that note, I extend my heartiest congratulations to all the award recipients of the Community Chest Awards.

Conclusion.

41

Honoring Winner of Award from United Negro College Fund

William L. Davis, R.R. Donnelley

Paula Banks received the Harold Hines Award presented by the United Negro College Fund. William L., Davis, former chairman, president, and CEO of R.R. Donnelly Company congratulated Ms. Banks at an awards ceremony on May 5, 2001. In his speech, he celebrates the current recipient of the award as well as names past honorees. The speaker talks about why such programs are important and how his own firm benefits from the program. The speech ends with an inspired use of a question, as if to imply the continuing nature of inquiry.

Scoping Document

Event:	First Annual Black and White Ball, United Negro College Fund
Theme:	Presentation of Harold Hines Award
Place:	Chicago, Illinois
Date:	May 5, 2001
Audience:	Approximately 1,000 conference attendees
Length:	About 5 minutes, 539 words

Speech

I am honored to be here tonight and, I think you'll agree, the folks at the United Negro College Fund know how to throw a party.

But more importantly, they know how to make a lifelong impact on the lives of students. Paula Banks is a classic example. Congratulations, Paula on receiving the Harold Hines Award which you so richly deserve.

Talking Points

A speech of congratulations is like a party.

But there's a serious side, too. Introduces the honoree and makes the congratulations explicit.

R.R. Donnelley has long supported the UNCF. But recently, through the scholar program, we have built an even stronger partnership with the organization. Each summer for the past two years, we've employed five student interns in our facilities here in Chicago and around the country. These students have been exceptional, garnering praise from supervisors and co-workers alike. In fact, the projects they get involved in are pretty impressive.

Introduces the relationship of the company to the awards.

Consider Rasheedah Hinskton from Fisk University who built a training and development website for our logistics services business . . .

Cites examples of success.

Or Marcus Belton from Benedict College who performed a detailed financial analysis for our direct mail advertising business.

There was also Kevin Jackson from Clark Atlanta and Georgia Institute of Technology who played a key role in the Continuous Improvement activities at one of our magazine plants.

I could go on, but you get the picture. And let me tell you, these kids are sharp. They often demonstrate their capabilities in ways you'd never expect.

Take Kevin Jackson, the young man I just mentioned. He was working on some process improvements in our Gallatin, Tennessee plant and had a question about a certain procedure he had to perform. Kevin didn't just go to his supervisor looking for an answer. He turned his quest for information into a test of our manufacturing people: Kevin asked five different people the same question to see if he would get five different answers.

Keeps giving examples.

I'm happy to say that we passed Kevin's test. All five of our people answered the same way. Good thing.

But the great thing about that story is Kevin, and the maturity and creativity he so often demonstrated during his internship. Thanks to the UNCF, there are many more students out there like Kevin who will get the chance to prove what they can do.

It's because of our experience with the scholar program that I volunteered to serve as a co-chairman of this inaugural gala. Let's keep the momentum going in the years to come.

I want to say thank you to some of the key people who made this event a success—my co-chairmen, Barbara and Jack, Marquis Miller and his UNCF team, and the UNCF Midwest Advisory Council, headed by R.R. Donnelley Executive Vice President Joe Lawler. An extra nod of thanks goes to the Midwest Advisory Council for conceiving this event and bringing it to life.

Spreads the thanks around.

Before I turn the podium over to Jack, I want to share a quote with you that struck a chord with me. It goes like this:

"An effective leader is an 'out-of-the-box' thinker, communicates well with others and is open to constructive criticism. The best results come from leading people, not managing them."

Quotation.

You know the person who said that? I just spoke about him. It's UNCF scholar Kevin Jackson. Not bad for a sophomore in college. What do you think?

Nice way to end the speech, quoting a college student. And ending a speech about college students with a question is inspired.

42

Traveling Companions: Commemorating 75 Years of Doing Business in Bartlesville

Wayne Allen, Phillips Petroleum

To express gratitude to the city of Bartlesville, Oklahoma, the city in which Phillips Petroleum does business, former president and chief operating officer Wayne Allen presented a restored, horse-drawn tank wagon to the city. In a ceremony to mark 75 years of doing business in Bartlesville, Allen presented the gift to the mayor of Bartlesville and other dignitaries.

Scoping Document

Event:	Community meeting
Theme:	Presentation of tank wagon to the city of Bartlesville
Place:	Johnstone Park, Bartlesville, Oklahoma
Date:	June 19, 1992
Audience:	Approximately 1,000 community members and Phillips employees
Length:	About 3 minutes, 389 words

Speech

Mayor Little, ladies and gentlemen of all ages: thanks for joining us for today's tank-wagon presentation ceremony.

It seems strange to think that the oil industry depended on horses for transportation back in the early days. But it's true. When tank wagons like this one were built, back around the turn of the century, there were almost no gasoline-powered vehicles on the road, except in a few big cities.

Talking Points

The speaker welcomes everyone.

When you got to the edge of town, there really weren't even any roads to speak of. As a matter of fact, oil tank wagons like this one helped build most of the early motor roads.

By 1908, the horse-drawn tank wagon was the principal means of transporting the asphalt used to pave our nation's growing network of roads and highways. By the time Phillips was founded in 1917, most horse-drawn wagons had been replaced by gasoline-powered trucks. So the vehicle in front of you is of considerable historical interest.

Adds history.

This particular tank wagon first saw duty in Kansas City and then spent many years at the Woolaroc Ranch. We had it completely restored in 1980. It's been used in various parades over the years since. But as of today, this tank wagon belongs to the City of Bartlesville, a gift from Phillips Petroleum, commemorating our 75 years of traveling together.

Tells the story of this specific tank wagon.

Announces dedication of the tank wagon to the people of Bartlesville.

Some of those roads have been pretty rough . . . haven't they Harvey? But even in tough times, Bartlesville has been a wonderful traveling companion. This town has been good to us. That's why we've stayed partners for three-quarters of a century. So, to express our appreciation, it is my great privilege and honor to present this Phillips 66 horse-drawn tank wagon to the city of Bartlesville. Here are the keys.

A personal question that emphasizes the ups and downs the company and the city have shared over the years.

Reaffirms the dedication of the tank wagon as an expression of the company's gratitude to the town.

The keys—as you may have guessed—are for the gate at the permanent shelter that's been built for the tank-wagon just across the road.

Having a key to actually hand over makes for a memorable photograph.

I'd also like to thank Ken Harris, the exhibit center supervisor for Phillips, who conceived the idea for this gift, and who managed the construction arrangements for the shelter. And I'd like to invite all of you to take a look at the facility while you're here.

Mayor Little, the wagon and the shelter are yours. We hope they will be an interesting attraction for the community for many years to come. Enjoy!

Completes the dedication.

ACCEPTANCES

Acceptance speeches represent one of the rare opportunities in business where it is appropriate, even preferred, to display some genuine emotion. Don't underestimate the emotional response you might feel when you are accepting the award and the audience stands up in applause. Don't fight it. You've earned it. The emotion is normal and desirable. The emotion is as much for the audience as it is for you. Organizations need to be able to celebrate. One way to do that is to appreciate individual contributors. So when the audience welcomes you to the podium, what do you say? Keep these points in mind.

- Start with a sincere opening comment.
- Share your personal feelings about receiving such an honor or gift.
- Refer, if appropriate, to the content of the presentation speech.
- Express your gratitude and acknowledge the audience.
- Thank the organization giving you the award and acknowledge the importance and value of the work they are doing.
- End with a heartfelt "thank you."

The goal of the acceptance speech is to offer gratitude for a gift or an award. Acceptance speeches are pretty easy unless you have difficulty in expressing gratitude. The award recipient's goal is to thank the individual or organization presenting the award and not do anything to make the audience reconsider the honor. The best way to do that is to share the credit (but not the award). By all means, recognize the people who helped you achieve the honor. Good acceptance speeches have these attributes:

- Short
- Gracious
- Sincere
- Credible
- Specific
- Appear impromptu

43

Together We Can Make a Difference

Dennis F. Strigl, Verizon

In these remarks Denny Strigl, executive vice president, Verizon Communications, and president and chief executive officer, Verizon Wireless, accepted an award for the company's contributions to combating domestic violence. In one of its early initiatives, the company distributed donated cell phones programmed to dial 911 to survivors of domestic violence. This speech marks the company's recognition for its HopeLine program.

Scoping Document

Event:	Mt. Sinai Silver Whistle Award
Theme:	NYC Victim Services' 2002 Champion Awards Luncheon
Place:	New York, New York
Date:	May 14, 2002
Audience:	Organization members, guests, dignitaries, media
Length:	About 3 minutes, 336 words

Speech

Thank you. On behalf of my 40,000 colleagues at Verizon Wireless, I wish to extend our gratitude to Mt. Sinai for this very special recognition.

Back in 1995, when my company decided to devote our community service efforts to domestic violence, many people asked "why?" — "Why not a cause that impacts more of the general population?"

Talking Points

Accepts award on behalf of the team.

Introduces a difficult subject by anticipating a question that some members of the audience might ask. This is a very effective technique to introduce the company's commitment to fighting domestic violence.

In that question, lies our challenge. Today, many people still do not see domestic violence as the epidemic it is.

Most of us in this room are aware that domestic violence is an epidemic. We may each see this issue from slightly different vantage points—as health care workers, or law enforcement officials, or television producers, or business managers, or caring neighbors. But what we all see the same is its very personal and terrible toll—on our patients, on our crime victims, on our coworkers, on our friends, our neighbors, our sisters, or daughters.

Again, the speaker aligns himself with the audience, acknowledging that there are different points of view.

Focuses on what all people can agree on.

From a business perspective alone, domestic violence has a devastating impact on employees in our own workforce who are being abused, on co-workers who work with the employee being abused and within the communities where we do business.

Addresses the reality that domestic violence is, among other things, a business issue that warrants the attention of responsible business leaders.

Domestic violence is pervasive, and it knows no socio- or economic boundaries. That is precisely why Verizon Wireless chose to put our resources and our wireless technology to work to combat domestic violence.

Elaborates on the issue.

And we chose to name our effort HopeLine, to embody the positive difference we intended to make in the areas of prevention and the life-rebuilding process.

Introduces the Verizon Wireless program that is being honored.

HopeLine started with the donation of voicemail boxes so victims could receive confidential messages from family and employers. It has grown into an army of initiatives, from HR guidelines, to bus posters and movie trailers, to the nationwide collection of phones to benefit domestic violence organizations exclusively.

Gives some context to HopeLine.

Tonight's Silver Whistle Awards are especially gratifying because they help raise overall awareness of domestic violence and its devastation . . . and they spotlight what each of us can do—whatever our walk of life—to make a difference.

Returns to the theme of the speech—accepting an award.

Concludes on a very personal and hopeful note.

CHAPTER 10

Speeches for Saying "Goodbye": Retirements, Farewells, Funerals and Eulogies, and Commencements

RETIREMENTS

One of the life-cycle events in any mature organization is the retirement of employees, founders, or key executives. It is traditional and fitting to acknowledge the services of these individuals with a celebration that calls for an individual representing the organization to deliver some remarks. Other examples of such speeches can be found under Farewells below and Tributes in Chapter 8.

Some retirement speeches are offered by the CEO or founder. Others come from the retirees themselves. There are no set rules for structuring retirement speeches. They can be humorous and whimsical or serious and weighty. Some are heavy on reminiscences. Others are forward-looking, exploring the new opportunities for the retired person. Most take time to acknowledge coworkers and express gratitude. The following speeches represent a spectrum of retirement remarks.

Trying to Be a Failure

John F. Budd, Jr., Emhart Corporation

Retirement speeches can be hilarious. In this speech celebrating the retirement of Wally Able, a valued employee of the Emhart Corporation, Chairman John F. Budd, Jr., took a satiric tone that cleverly noted the honoree's many successes without getting sentimental about it. Sustaining this level of satire is very difficult, but there's not a false note in this speech.

Scoping Document

Event:	Wally Able retirement party
Theme:	Trying to Be a Failure
Place:	Emhart Corporation headquarters
Date:	July 29, 1983
Audience:	Employees
Length:	About 5 minutes, 502 words

Speech

We're here, you think, to honor Wally Able for his success. That's all wrong! This may be news to each of you, but Wally didn't want to be a success at all. He's been trying to be a failure.

Don't laugh. Failure is a subject of great importance. Isn't an American citizen supposed to have freedom of choice?

Things are so arranged in our society today that it is increasingly hard to become a full-fledged failure. Especially if you go to college. You've all seen it. A man like Wally Able, with all the makings of a perfect failure, suddenly he's swept to success just because he got overconfident.

Talking Points

A challenging opening suggests this speech is not business as usual.

Tongue in cheek all the way.

242

Let me tell you—it requires as much practice and skill to become a truly outstanding failure as it does to become truly great in any field.

First, of course, you have to rid yourself of that almost universal belief that success is desirable. That's what trapped Wally right at the outset. We can probably blame his weakness on Worchester Poly. They brainwashed him when he was young and impressionable and planted the virus of ambition.

Everything the speaker says is intended to be taken as its opposite.

Happiness and success are not synonymous.

Happiness, you see, is to be chasing madly after something you really want, with the hope of catching it—*someday*!

Where Wally went wrong was he chased things—*and caught them*. He had success—but *not happiness* . . .

Successes, he also found out, worked like dogs. Failures don't work at all.

Successes get so wound up in their jobs they can't sleep, even counting microchips . . . failures can always sleep—even in the daytime.

By now the audience is rolling in the aisles.

If you're a success, Wally learned, your problems get bigger and bigger. You have to learn to adjust to the trauma of having a staff of 720 one day—and zero the next . . . or trying to make money in atomic energy.

Always brings it back to the honoree.

To my knowledge, there isn't one government agency, church or private institution devoted to the care and treatment of successful people. On the other hand, if you're a failure of any variety—everybody worries about you and wants to take care of you. It's the American love for the underdog—no matter how far under.

The biggest tactical error Wally Able made in his business working days was when he fell in love with his work. The real enemy of failure is the thrill of achievement. Because they discovered achievement is fun, more promising failures like Wally have gone wrong than for any other single reason.

Shares the secrets of Wally Able's success.

Part of the original sin of the human race is this compulsion . . . this deep-grounded desire for achievement. I wish we understood it!!!

This is what made man fly faster than birds, dive deeper than fish, sent man to the moon and kept Wally Able from failing for 44 years.

Notes the honoree's tenure of 44 years.

It's too late, now, for Wally, but for the rest of us maybe there's a chance.

But, Beware . . . watch out for that moment when, as Wally learned, pride begins to creep into your work. Achievement is not dangerous to failure . . . *except* when you do it on the job.

Remember what happened to the man we commiserate with this evening. He could have been a truly great failure—in fact, an outstanding one. He tried hard—like when he tried to introduce a synthetic leather shoe—or the baseball stitching machine—but in the end, he aimed too high . . . his dreams were too big.

Above all, ignore, forget, and never, never repeat what a man named James Barrie once said—

"Work is never work unless there is something else you'd rather be doing." | *Quotation from the author of "Peter Pan."*

It took Wally Able a helluva long time to accept this advice. | *Irreverent conclusion to an irreverent but charming speech.*

FAREWELLS

Although the turnover in modern business has obviously increased the opportunities for making farewell speeches, the practice of making formal farewell speeches is much restricted. At the same time, the need for informal farewell remarks increases with each set of layoffs.

If you are leaving the organization, it is appropriate in your farewell remarks to

- Give a brief explanation for why you are leaving
- Express affection for the organization
- Recall memorable or exciting projects
- Summarize major accomplishments
- Tell brief anecdotes
- Let listeners know you will remember them
- Promise to stay in touch or visit
- Thank those you are leaving and wish them luck

If someone else is leaving, and you are called on to make a farewell speech on that person's behalf, the most important thing for you to know is why the person is leaving. In your remarks, it is appropriate for you to

- Let the audience know what the occasion is all about
- Express regret tempered with best wishes for luck and success
- Thank the person leaving with specific praise for specific accomplishments
- Share brief anecdotes
- Get as personal as the relationship allows
- Evoke a feeling of unity or family
- Wish the person well and invite him or her to visit

If you or another person is leaving the organization under unfavorable circumstances, don't worry. There simply won't be a farewell speech, ceremony, or public acknowledgment. In any case, in business farewell speeches all parties should avoid

- Slamming the door
- Criticizing others
- Defending oneself
- Effusive praise
- Over-the-top sentimentality

It Has Been One Hell of a Ride

Lee Iacocca, Chrysler

Lee Iacocca retired after 14 tumultuous years at Chrysler. During his tenure, the very survival of the company was in question, salvaged only by a highly controversial loan guarantee from the federal government. But through it all, Iacocca led with candor, and that willingness to confront the bad news directly was evident in his farewell remarks to over 1,400 top managers who crowded into the new Chrysler Technology Center in Auburn, Michigan. He began, as usual, with a joke. "Sorry so many of you have to stand. Maybe we should have built this dining room a little bigger! But we couldn't afford it!"

Scoping Document

Event:	Senior management meeting
Theme:	Saying goodbye to Lee Iacocca
Place:	Chrysler Facility, Auburn Hills, Michigan
Date:	November 18, 1992
Audience:	Approximately 1,400 senior managers
Length:	About 8 minutes, 847 words

Speech

I asked for this meeting today. If you came thinking I had some big announcement today, or even to talk business, then I got you here under false pretenses.

This is personal.

I asked you here because, as you all know, I'm getting to be a short-timer. I've worked in the auto industry for 46 years . . . 2 months . . . 3 weeks . . . and 3 days. And in another six weeks and one day, it's time for me to get out of here.

Talking Points

Informal beginning to what could be a maudlin event signals how Iacocca wants to handle it: stay upbeat.

Sets up the tone even more directly.

But who's counting?

I've got a lot of things to do before I clean out the office, but nothing more important than what I want to do today.

And that's simply to say thanks . . . thanks to every one of you.

In every farewell speech, thanks must be the key organizing principle.

That's the only reason I wanted to meet with you today—just to say thanks. For almost two months now, I've been thanking everybody else—the shareholders in May, the dealers in August, the bankers, the financial analysts, suppliers, the press, the employees at Warren truck, and here at the tech center all day today, and I finally got around to management role—1,400 of you!

People keep asking me how I feel about retiring. Well, I feel good, and I also feel bad.

Asking a question he wants to answer.

I feel good, first of all, because Chrysler is in great shape. I couldn't leave three years ago when my tour of duty was up because we had problems. Some of them were created by forces over which we had no control. Some of them we created ourselves.

Addresses the upside.

But I was in the corner office, so I had to accept the responsibility for getting the place back in shape.

But I know, and I hope every one of you know, where the real credit belongs. And that, of course, is to you.

Takes the opportunity to describe and thank the management team.

If I had left three years ago, I'd have had to walk away from a job that wasn't finished. I'm not built that way. And now, thanks to all of you, I can walk away proud of what I'm leaving behind.

Follows this statement with a series of stories whose effect is to praise Lee Iacocca, something the speaker would never do directly.

Now, regrets, yeah, I have a few.

Addresses the downside in a series of specific, candid statements.

I regret having had to close 32 plants on my watch. Closing a plant is the hardest thing a CEO ever has to do. It hurts, and it hurts deeply.

I regret not having the time to make some of the changes we had to do more slowly and with less pain. But we didn't have that luxury.

I wish that we had improved our quality faster and closed in on the Japanese faster than we did.

I wish I could take back a model or two. They weren't all hits.

I wish I'd never heard of odometers.

A reference to the odometer roll-back scandal (see Speech 24).

I wish I'd stop getting letters from customers with complaints about the way they've been treated by dealers—especially the women.

Those are the regrets.

There are a lot of other things we did that our critics told us we'd regret, but the critics were wrong.

Transitions back to some upside statements, but notice it's not what Iacocca is proud of, it's what he does not regret.

I don't regret the billion dollars we invested in this place, even though we had to mortgage the whole amount at what turned out to be junk bond rates.

I don't regret spending another billion to build the new Jefferson plant. I sure don't regret buying American Motors.

We took some big risks. And they were worth it.

Since I've been counting down the days, a couple of people on my staff have been making lists. They tell me that since I came to Chrysler, we've built (and sold) 25 million vehicles.

Well, we've been through hell again and we're heroes again. The papers just a year ago said that we were a bunch of stumblebums who didn't know our left from our right. Now, they're raving about our new products and the fact that we're the only people in town making money.

I just want to wind up with one last request. It's an important one.

I want all of you to give Bob Eaton the same kind of support you've given me over the years. I envy him and I envy you because, if you take the free advice I just gave you, the best of times are still to come for Chrysler.

And I've got one hope for Bob Eaton.

A few weeks ago, I was on the morning news shows, and all the interviewers asked me what my biggest accomplishment was at Chrysler.

I had to tell them the truth. I said it was simply survival. The company survived.

My hope is that when they ask Bob Eaton the same question when he retires, he won't have to say "survival." I hope we've put that part of our history behind us.

It's time to move on.

What follows is a series of statistics demonstrating how Chrysler has grown under Iacocca's leadership (omitted here).

Transition to a more personal account of Chrysler.

Concludes by asking for support for his successor, Bob Eaton. Such a request is virtually a requirement for a farewell speech.

Transition to conclusion. Short statements signal a dramatic end.

We've got the leadership to do that.

It's a new and better era for Chrysler. Please make the most of it.

All in all, it has been one hell of a ride!

In fact, if I had known that it was going to be this exciting at Chrysler, I would have pissed off Henry Ford a lot sooner than I did!

Can't resist a final joke. Iacocca came to Chrysler after a falling out with Henry Ford at Ford Motor Co.

Thanks for making that ride possible.

Let's go get a drink.

This conclusion might have worked in 1992, but it's probably not appropriate in a formal business speech today.

46 Thank You for This Wonderful Send-Off

John Kador

The speech is a classic example of a tightly focused, wistful farewell speech with just a hint of satisfaction. The images it offers are precise and situated squarely in the DNA of the company. Its appeal to gratitude is sincere without being maudlin. The length is perfect, the rhythm flows to an applause line, and there is not a false note in the speech.

Scoping Document

Event: Farewell ceremony

Theme: Bidding farewell to employee

Place: Conference room in the Midwest

Date: Anytime

Audience: Coworkers

Length: About 3 minutes, 300 words

Speech

Bidding farewell to so many friends is the most difficult thing I've ever been asked to do for this wonderful organization.

You've all meant a great deal to me personally and professionally.

From you I learned this business of ours. From you I learned a vast technology.

But I also learned much more.

Talking Points

The speaker doesn't mince words about the subject of the speech. The audience relaxes in knowing this speech will be positive.

The human connection.

The "but" indicates a turn to the serious.

I took my PhD here in ethics and decency, in understanding and encouragement.

What a glowing compliment to the organization.

I am leaving you now, but I will take with me into a new phase of my career absolutely everything you have taught me.

And I'll be taking much than a collection of virtues and lessons, however valuable they are. I'll also take memories of Brad, my supervisor for the last five years, who taught me so much about not only database administration but the delights of fly fishing.

Offers very concrete memories. Mentions a few names.

Monday mornings will never be the same for me without the aroma of the freshly baked bread that Ingrid brings every Monday.

Invokes other senses: the sense of smell can be very powerful.

And I'll never forget the tugs-of-war between IT and sales.

Alludes, gently, to some friction.

I would be disingenuous if I didn't acknowledge that I am totally psyched by the prospect of moving to a new place and starting something I've worked toward for a long time. But it is like leaving your family; something in the course of life you have to do, but something that's not easier for having to do it.

Here's the "Don't cry for me" reference.

Thank you for this wonderful, generous send-off.

I will keep in touch by email, and every time I travel back to this beautiful area, I will let you know.

This promise to keep in touch is mandatory. No one expects follow-through.

Meanwhile, I take comfort in the fact that we are living in an increasingly connected world. The chances of us meeting and working together again have never been better. I wish you all the best.

It has been a treat to know you all.

A "treat." People who heard this speech will not soon forget it.

47

You Had Me at Hello

John Kador

We can call him Tim Andrews. Where he worked and what he did really don't matter. What we know is that he was a superstar, one of those employees you never want to see leave, but you know they must and are probably better off for doing so. Nevertheless, all you can do, if you are Tim's supervisor, is what this speaker does: praise him to the skies and make sure he knows he is welcome back. Every farewell speech offers praise. This one frames the praise in terms of the bright future this employee will have. The length of these remarks is ideal as is the tone of massive congratulations and ever-so-slight regret.

Scoping Document

Event:	Employee farewell ceremony
Theme:	Beloved employee leaves company
Place:	Anywhere
Date:	Anytime
Audience:	Fellow coworkers
Length:	About 2 minutes, 223 words

Speech

You might remember a line from the film *Jerry Maguire.*

The heroine tells the hero, "You had me at hello."

That's the way we all feel about Tim Andrews, who we are all gathered to send off with our best wishes.

Let me be frank.

Talking Points

Startling opening bound to get the audience's attention . . .

. . . especially if they saw the movie.

Takes the liberty of speaking for the group, which is what a leader does.

As a transition this can be effective, but it sets up the vague

*unease that other statements, not
similarly prefaced, may be less
than frank.*

There are employees we absolutely hate to leave us,
and there are those about whose departure we are
more indifferent.

Timothy Andrews is the poster boy for the first
category.

*Makes clear how the speaker
thinks of the honoree.*

Tim, I am so very proud of all that you have accomplished here, all that you have given us, all that will
stay with us after you are gone.

*Direct statement of affection.
It's one thing to speak for the
audience. The speaker must also
speak for him or herself.*

I am also proud that you are leaving us to take on a
position of so much responsibility and potential. I
know that you will do very excellent things in your
new job.

We will read about you in the trade magazines.

*Looks into the future to pour on
the praise.*

We will point to you with pride as we say, "Timothy
Andrews got his start right here."

*The speaker could have looked at
past accomplishments, as well.*

Tim, it's been an honor to work with you, break
bread with you, and watch you flourish.

Rule of three.

You know I wish you the best of luck, but I'd be
lying if I said I don't hate to see you go.

*Here's that frankness again.
It's good to acknowledge such
feelings.*

Take care of yourself and wherever your brilliant
career will take you, just know that you always have
a home here.

*Offers the opportunity to come
back.*

FUNERALS AND EULOGIES

According to most surveys, public speaking is the number one fear that people have. Death is number two. I've never believed that particular piece of urban legend. If true, it would mean that more people would rather be the one in the casket than the one giving the eulogy. That's not to take away from the anxiety of public speaking. A eulogy is a public speech that is usually (but not always) given in praise of a person at funerals or memorial services.

When someone important to an organization dies, the organization cannot really move on until a leader acknowledges the event and creates some meaning around it. That is the job of a business leader. In addition to fulfilling a critical business function, delivering a eulogy is also an indispensable part of the healing process. The best advice in preparing a eulogy is to be direct. Everyone knows why you are up there, so get right to it. No one expects you to make the pain go away. All they want is a little comfort and to have some context for their mixed feelings. Here are some attributes to strive for:

- Address the person by name. "Ben Stone often said . . ."
- Speak from personal experience.
- Admit feelings of grief. If you will miss the deceased say so.
- Emphasize the unity of feeling in the room.
- Use quotes from deceased.
- Reminisce about early years of the deceased.
- Speak honestly. Include a balanced look at the person's life.
- Pay attention to the rhythm of your remarks.
- Relieve tension with anecdotes or humor.
- Keep your ego out of it.
- Reach out to everyone in the audience, not just coworkers.
- Weave background information into the stories you tell.
- Be inclusive by quoting long-time friends and colleagues.
- Write from the heart.
- End on an emotional appeal.
- Keep it short—don't make the audience envy the deceased.

Eulogies are fragile things. You can preserve their dignity by avoiding these gaffes:

- Abstractions and clichés.
- Euphemisms—The person died. He didn't go to his "great reward" or the "paperless office in the sky."
- Rhetoric—"Who can discern the mysteries of life and death?"
- Aspersions of the deceased or his character.
- Dwelling on death, pain, or misery.
- Commenting on the senselessness or tragedy of death—all deaths are tragic.

48 You Went Too Far This Time

John Kador

> *This effusive eulogy is by a younger employee marking the passing of a mentor. In its praise and willingness to address the deceased directly, the speaker not only lets the audience feel the grief and loss, but uses a bit of irreverence to give the audience some breathing room.*

Scoping Document

Event:	Eulogy
Theme:	Saying goodbye to a beloved coworker
Place:	Anywhere
Date:	Anytime
Audience:	Coworkers, friends, family
Length:	About 4 minutes, 372 words

Speech

We live in times of great complexity and are beset by far-reaching problems. We will not greatly err if upon every such occasion we consult the genius of Ben Stone, whom death has taken from us.

I love the Ben Stone story we tell about the time he was asked to give a speech.

As Ben reviewed the first draft, he noticed that his speechwriter indicated "cheers" to describe the audience's reaction. Ben took a pencil and scratched out the word *cheers*. The speechwriter was suitably impressed by what he thought was an unusual display of modesty. But then Ben replaced what he scratched out with "loud and prolonged applause."

Talking Points

A eulogy written in the literary tradition.

Anecdotes about the deceased are always welcome. But make sure it's an upper.

259

Ben was not modest in life, and we needn't be modest about him in death.

This is the main theme of the eulogy.

Ben Stone refused to categorize people. That's the first thing I noticed about him when he hired me.

Important for the speaker at a eulogy to identify the relationship.

I was just out of the service. My friends called me "Sarge," but Ben simply didn't pigeonhole me. He regarded each and every person he met as a unique, multifaceted, complex human being with a unique background and unique gifts to bring to bear.

Now I'm supposed to stand up here and do to Ben what he refused to do to anyone else, and I won't do it.

A challenge to tradition.

It's tempting to describe Ben with the kinds of words and phrases that he would never use to describe anyone else. All the words you can think of—genius, splendid, curious, helpful, yearning—are true enough. All these words are true enough, but he was much more than what little they convey.

Ben, you really went a little too far this time. We know you would use any excuse to gather your best friends into one room! But excuse us if, on balance, we would rather forgo the get-together and have you with us for a few more years.

Addressing the deceased directly gives the eulogy an almost unbearable poignancy.

This time, you've gone too far. Much too far, and I miss you already. I miss your kind words and the advice you refused to give until I had it figured out for myself.

Restatement of the main theme.

You were the best mentor I ever had, and I hope I can repay my debt to you by being half as good a mentor to someone else.

Effusive close.

49

A Wonderful, Caring Friend to the Working Person

John Kador

This upbeat, folksy yet edgy eulogy was delivered by the grandson of the deceased, William Timsdale Everitt, the founder of Tricity Textiles, a textile manufacturing firm in the Northeast. The speech keeps the audience riveted because it swings wildly between a traditional, almost sentimental eulogy and an almost post-modern black comedy.

Scoping Document

Event:	Company and community meeting
Theme:	Eulogy for company founder
Place:	Tricity Textiles company headquarters
Date:	January 30, 2003
Audience:	Family, coworkers, retirees, members of the community
Length:	About 6 minutes, 617 words

Speech

On behalf of Tricity Textiles, I'd like to thank you all for coming here this morning.

Our founder, William Timsdale Everitt, died on January 15, 2003. Tim, as he was called by everyone from the chairman of the board to the line, was born in Brooklyn in June of 1902 and lived for 101 years.

He lived through a time of almost unimaginable change.

To put it into perspective, when Tim was born, one of his immigrant father's jobs was lighting the gas

Talking Points

Welcoming the group is important.

Naming the deceased is important.

Concrete example illustrating change.

lamps in the streets of New York. By the time he died peacefully in his sleep, his children, grandchildren, and great-grandchildren bathed in the cool light of their computer monitors.

Tim married young, and stayed married to my grandma, Edna, for 60 years, until her passing in 1989. He had two children. The eldest, his daughter Sally, died young of an infection, one that could have been easily cured just a few years later, after the invention of penicillin. His second child was my father, Joe.

Speaker identifies his relationship to the deceased.

Like so many others, the family struggled through hard times.

My grandfather worked for the phone company until he was laid off during the Depression, and then he got a job with a bank appraising houses. When the Depression finally ended, Western Electric hired him back, first in Philadelphia and then in New Jersey.

After World War II, Tim founded TriCity Textiles. From the beginning, the company prospered and thanks to his leadership, it grew to its present size, employing over 1,000 people in three plants across the area. TriCity Textiles is the largest employer in the county.

We remember the Christmas Fire of 1961, when the Tarrytown plant—the oldest of the three—burned down three days before Christmas. Tim didn't have to think about what to do. He could have split up the 550 workers, sending some on long commutes to the other plants, furloughing the rest. But that was not Tim's way.

Recounts one of the key unifying events of the company.

He kept everyone—and I mean everyone—on full salary until the plant was rebuilt.

There was a fabulous party to celebrate the reopening of the plant. I'm told I was there. I don't remember much about that night. It's said that if you remember the celebration, you weren't there.

The eulogy is moving from the traditional to the postmodern, with a bit of irreverence.

That's Tim. A wonderful, caring friend to the working person who would give you the shirt off his back.

He had a large capacity for life, for song, for intricate meals. Some of you dined at his home and knew of his strange, experimental cooking. The recipe for peppermint wiener schnitzel with pistachio nuts thankfully goes with him to the grave.

A little edgy here.

Family always came before business to Tim. When Joe and my mother, Dorothy, moved to California in 1961, Tim and my grandmother regularly drove across the country to visit. Corporate jets weren't for him. After he retired he moved closer to us and I got to spend a lot of good fishing days with him until just a short time ago.

Eulogy moves back to sentimentality.

Tim wasn't always the easiest person to get along with. He had very definite opinions—covering just about everything. Everyone in the family has a memory of the time Tim questioned their opinions or choice in mates. Some would call him outspoken. Others would call him blunt. Still, he could be very generous with gifts for his family.

Back to edgy. These transitions keep the audience guessing.

No doubt it is easy to feel sorry at a funeral: sorry for the departed one; sorry for the grieving family; sorry for oneself. I'm sorry, too.

Classy conclusion.

Let me tell you whom I feel sorry for most. I feel sorry for the many people who did not have the rare and wonderful opportunity of meeting, of knowing, of working with William Timsdale Everitt.

Honors the subject of the speech by closing the speech with the name of the person being honored.

COMMENCEMENTS

"Speeches in our culture are the vacuum that fills a vacuum," says John Kenneth Galbraith. Every Spring, hundreds of universities and colleges invite business people to address the graduates. Since the colleges understand that business has a bigger influence on the lives of people than ever before, it is understandable that they want business people to give advice. Resist the temptation to do so. Students don't want advice and, unlike employees, will not hesitate to show you how little they want it. After four years of classes, they don't want another lecture. They want to be entertained, and briefly. Inspiration is extra. The best commencement speeches don't take themselves too seriously. They are humorous, personal, offer one or two main points, promise brevity and then deliver on the promise.

It's a Free-Flight World Out There

Tom Weidemeyer, United Parcel Service

When Embry-Riddle University, the nation's best-known university for training pilots, looked for a commencement speaker, it turned to an executive of one of the world's big airlines: United Parcel Service Airlines, the 11th largest airline in the world. UPS welcomes commencement speeches for its executives because the company nurtures relationships, in this case with the highly trained graduates who will fly and maintain the company's aircraft. "We have a long history with the university, and we saw this as both a way to give back to the school and to also position our executives and our brand in a thoughtful way," says an executive speechwriter for UPS. Tom Weidemeyer, chief operating officer of United Parcel Service and president of UPS Airlines, responded with a commencement address in which he actually attempted something most contemporary commencement speakers resist doing: He offered genuine advice. But he did so in such an engaging style, using references to popular culture such as Homer Simpson, that the advice works. Weidemeyer encouraged the students to think about their aviation careers as a mission rather than as a job. He also cautioned graduates not to be consumed by work, but rather to keep their work life and home life in balance. Throughout it all, he gave subtle plugs to UPS and its culture.

Scoping Document

Event:	College commencement
Theme:	Aviation can be a mission rather than a job
Place:	Embry-Riddle University, Daytona Beach, Florida
Date:	April 27, 2002
Audience:	Students and their families, faculty, guests
Length:	About 18 minutes, 1,705 words

Speech

Good morning!

Now you can tell your grandchildren that George Thorogood played at your college commencement!

That little UPS commercial debuted right next door at the Daytona 500 this past February. It's the last UPS plug you're going to hear in this address.

But the idea of "Brown to the Bone" . . . the concept that you could love your job and get excited about your company . . .

. . . Well, you're going to hear a bit more about this a little later.

First, let me say that it's an honor to address the Embry-Riddle graduating class of 2002.

I have to tell you, I feel a lot of pressure right now.

There are about 300 Embry-Riddle graduates . . . pilots . . . engineers . . . and aviation specialists . . . who work for UPS Airlines.

And they all warned me not to be boring.

They went on to suggest that I be funny.

They even told me to be inspirational.

Talking Points

The speaker sets the stage.

George Thorogood had a hit with "Bad to the Bone," which UPS reworked as "Brown to the Bone" to support its new branding campaign in a commercial first aired during the Daytona 500, across the street from Embry-Riddle University.

Emphasizing the new UPS branding campaign.

Here's the formal start of the speech.

Gets personal right away.

Establishes long-term connection between the university and UPS.

Pace of speech accelerates with three "they" statements.

Well, I can't be everything at once. So, I chose to go the inspirational route. I figured, hey, I'm a lawyer. We lawyers inspire a lot of things in a lot of people!

I looked up some inspirational quotes from some leading minds.

I turned first to the great writer and thinker, Homer.

Homer Simpson.

Homer says there are three little sentences that will get you through life:

1. "Cover for me."
2. "Oh, good, idea, Boss!" And
3. "It was like that when I got here."

As you might have expected, I decided to continue with my research.

For even better ideas, I started thumbing through a brochure for the Embry-Riddle College of Aviation Complex.

I noticed a section about the future of aviation . . . and how the concept of "free flight" will eventually be adopted by global air-traffic control systems.

As you know, free flight will allow pilots and airlines to set their own routes . . . take advantage of favorable winds and weather . . . burn less fuel . . . and shorten flights.

Announcing the intention to be inspirational is tricky. If you say it, you have to deliver. And if you deliver, you don't have to say it.

Captures the audience's attention with a little sleight of hand: offering the Greek poet and storyteller and then invoking the TV cartoon character of the same name.

Rule of three works beautifully here.

Transition.

Introduces aviation concept of "free flight" as a metaphor for career choices.

"As you know . . ." The tried and true formula for speakers who need to give an explanation.

Collision-avoidance systems will provide a protective bubble around each plane. They'll alter the plane's speed and position to prevent mid-air collisions.

By setting pilots free to make their own common-sense choices . . . we will be able to speed travel, relieve congestion, improve safety, and cut costs.

I got to thinking more about free flight.

Isn't the freedom to make sensible choices what life is all about?

Question to be answered.

And that's what I want to talk to you about today:

Emphasizes that this is, indeed, the main theme of the speech.

About applying the concept of free flight to your careers and to your lives.

Makes the metaphor explicit.

About making the right choices in your careers.

Repeats the main theme.

Take it from someone who's lived a little longer than you:

It's always a risk to invoke seniority, but the speaker gets away with it here.

Your life largely ends up being the sum of the choices you make.

There's an old proverb that says:

"There is a choice you have to make, in everything you do. You must always keep in mind that the choices you make . . . make you."

Better to identify source of quotation.

I really believe that. You make choices. But your choices also make you.

Restatement of theme.

The fears you face. . .

Gives examples of choices in rhythm of three.

The risks you take. . .

How you treat people . . . the little, momentary decisions you make to do right or do wrong:

These are the choices that move you—impercepti-bly—in one direction or another . . . until you look around and notice you are a long way from where you started.

To the 2002 graduates of Embry-Riddle, I say: good start!

Brings attention back to the moment.

By attending the world's preeminent university dedi-cated to aviation, you have demonstrated that you know exactly what you want to do with your life.

This at a time when many people your age are still trying to decide on their majors.

You have chosen wisely. Now, more than ever, the world needs your skills, talents, education, enthusi-asm and passion.

In the wake of 9/11, we all suffered a major blow. The aviation industry felt it more than most. In fact, I think we can make the argument that this has been the most tumultuous year in the history of aviation.

Adds context by referring to the central trauma of the age.

And as the nation rediscovered its inner strength, we also rediscovered the critical role of aviation in global commerce.

Without a free-flowing aviation system, trade is stran-gled and economies suffocate.

Air cargo volume alone accounts for almost a third of world trade in merchandise.

We also learned that our citizens are not really free unless they have full confidence in the safety of our aviation system.

All that said, you are entering the workforce at a time of unparalleled challenge . . . but it's also a time of extraordinary opportunity.

A time when purposeful leadership can calm fears.

When knowledge can trump uncertainty.

When new ideas can triumph over old grievances.

You have chosen to make your career in aviation.

Transition to discussion of career choices, which the speaker hopes will include UPS.

It is my hope that you'll continue to make good choices, large and small.

In the spirit of free flight, it's all up to you.

Evokes metaphor of free flight.

Here's one big choice you'll have to make:

You'll have to decide whether you want to go to a job . . . or go on a mission.

You go to a job because you have to. You go on a mission because you want to.

Let me tell you what I've observed:

Gets personal.

I've watched new pilots and engineers and aviation specialists start their careers with great gusto.

They are passionate about what they do . . .

they can't wait to apply what they've learned . . .

and they're determined to make a difference.

These are the kinds of people who would probably love that "Brown to the Bone" song.

Unfortunately, after five or six years on the job, I've also seen a few of these same people lose their passion for their work.

They still do their jobs, and they still perform well . . . but I sense that they might care more about work schedules and vacation time than they do about flying.

That's when a mission downgrades into a job. I urge you to try to maintain the same kind of passion for aviation that John Paul Riddle carried with him his entire life.

As an Air Corp cadet in Arcadia, Florida, in the early 1920s . . . Mr. Riddle was supposed to be limited to only five hours of flying time a month because of budget restrictions.

Personalizes the speech by telling a story about the founder of Embry-Riddle University.

Well, since some of the other air cadets were more interested in nearby beach diversions than in getting in their flying time . . . the co-founder of Embry-Riddle was able to take their hours and log more flying time than any other cadet on the field.

Until his death in 1989, Mr. Riddle retained his love for aviation . . . frequently visiting this campus and talking enthusiastically with students like yourselves.

I understand that you could sense this same kind of passion if you worked with one 1983 Embry-Riddle graduate in particular.

Invokes another graduate and ties his story to 9/11 and the issue of making choices.

A gentleman by the name of David Charlebois.

Before David died when the hijacked American Airlines jet he was piloting hurtled into the side of the Pentagon . . . he was known as someone who loved what he did.

He was always trying to convince his nervous aunt that the skies were the safest place in the world.

He liked to talk about how beautiful the angles were when you were heading up through the clouds.

And he always carried a set of tools with him onboard. After the mechanics made their sweep, David would double-check the plane himself.

People like David Charlebois and John Paul Riddle were on a mission.

I'm not implying that you absolutely must feel 100 percent gung-ho every single hour . . . of every single day . . . of your career.

But passion is a choice.

If you choose to see your job as a mission . . . from day one until the day you retire . . . you'll never quit loving it.

Of course, the very word "mission" implies the job you do will have an impact on others. It's hard to maintain passion for your job when you are only focused on yourself and your own personal goals.

It's true that you can be too consumed by work. That's why it's important to keep your work life and your home life in balance.

Easier said than done, believe me.

But I promise you . . . as much as you love aviation . . . and as much as you'll love your jobs . . . no one here on their death bed will be wishing they had spent more time at work. I also don't know anyone who keeps their boss' picture in their wallet.

Advice that most graduates rarely hear.

Your work is your work . . . and it can be fulfilling and exhilarating.

But it's important to be part of something bigger than yourself.

Spend your time away from work connecting with the people, places and things . . . that make you a complete individual. Family . . . community . . . life-long learning. Those experiences, by the way, will only help you on the job.

Jim Casey . . . the gentleman who started the company I work for way back in 1907 really believed in this concept and its impact on teamwork.

The man who first tried sending packages via airplanes in the late 1920s always appreciated the role of aviation in global commerce.

Jim Casey told of looking out the window of an airplane many years later. He was looking out and marveling at the accomplishments of man below. Jim said he was reminded of how small any one person is in the grand scheme of things. And how people really have to work together to accomplish great things.

Ladies and gentlemen: It's a free-flight world out there.

Transition to closing by restating the metaphor.

You can either choose to follow the advice of people like Homer Simpson, who once advised his daughter:

"Lisa, if you don't like your job, you don't strike. You just go in every day and do it really half-baked. That's the American way."

Or you can make the choice that will make your life's journey smoother and faster:

You can choose to see your career in aviation as a mission . . . to be part of something bigger than yourself . . . to go to work every day because you want to, not because you have to.

Congratulations, and Bon Voyage!

Symmetry of closing by invoking Homer Simpson again.

Elegant conclusion.

List of Contributors and Resources

For the speechwriter in need of tools, information, or inspiration, the Internet has resources in abundance. The following individuals and organizations were especially helpful to me in the preparation of this book. Chances are good they will be as helpful to you.

Organizational Resources

The Executive Speaker Company

The Executive Speaker Library is an extraordinary resource for speechwriters interested in business speeches. The Speech Library includes the full texts of over 6,600 speeches by executives that have been indexed on any of over 4,000 keywords. Speeches may be searched by special occasions, such as retirement, commencement, ethics, theme-based meetings, and humor. The speeches are also indexed on speaker's name, company or organization, and audience. For people who need a speech, the website includes a list of recommended business speechwriters. The subscription-based service offers a number of newsletters. *Executive Speaker*, a monthly newsletter, includes openings, closings, and pointmakers from recent speeches by executives. *Executive Speeches*, a bimonthly journal, includes full texts of the best recent speeches by executives. *Quote . . . Unquote*, a quarterly newsletter, provides authoritative information on the origin, history, and meaning of quotations, slogans, proverbs, and proverbial expressions. Contact the publisher Robert O. Skovgard, at speaker@toast.net or (937) 294-8493 for subscription rates. http://www.executive-speaker.com

Speechwriter's Newsletter

Speechwriter's Newsletter, is just one of the resources available to speechwriters at www.ragan.com. The monthly newsletter offers tips, answers questions, provides topical quotes, and a "this month in history" section. In addition, subscribers can take advantage of a Listserve and a speechwriters' forum. Contact David Murray, editor at dmurrayil@earthlink.net or Lawrence Ragan Communications, Inc., (800) 493-4867.

National Speaker's Association

The National Speaker's Association (NSA) is the leading organization for experts who speak professionally. NSA's 4,000 members include speakers, writers, trainers, educators, humorists, motivators, consultants, authors, and more. Check out the Knowledge Bank and Resource Center at www.nsaspeaker.org.

Say It Better Center

With the theme of "communicate to connect" this website offers a growing collection of free articles and electronic as well as traditional books on how to improve one's communication skills.

For more information contact Kare Anderson at kare@sayitbetter.com or (800) 488-KARE (5273). www.sayitbetter.com

IdeaBank

IdeaBank is a subscription-based database of quotations, anecdotes, book and speech excerpts, proverbs, humor, and other material that can be used to make verbal and written communications more memorable. www.idea-bank.com

H&K INK: The Writers Group

The H&K Writers Group is a service of Hill & Knowlton Public Affairs Worldwide. It offers a team from journalism, government, and the arts to craft the right words, expressed in the right style, to convey ideas effectively in speeches, Op-Ed commentaries, congressional testimony, policy "white papers," and journal articles.

Contact Senior Vice President Christopher Colford at ccolford@hillandknowlton.com.

TheSpeechwriter.com

TheSpeechwriter.com is a feature-rich resource organized by Fletcher Dean, a speechwriter for a *Fortune* 500 company, who also has a freelance practice. The site has among the deepest resources for speechwriters, including tools such as a variety of dictionaries and links to other services. Best of all, it's free.

Contact Fletcher Dean at fletcher@thespeechwriter.com. www.thespeechwriter.com

Independent Speechwriters Specializing in Business Speeches

Ken Askew

A freelance speechwriter and strategic executive communication consultant
kenaskew@aol.com

William Bartlett

East Coast–based corporate speechwriter
wvbart@yahoo.com

Craig L. Howe

craig.howe@greatfallsgroup.com

Eugene Finerman

Whether from abundant talent or immature ambivalence, Eugene Finerman is a speechwriter and humorist.
finerman@theramp.net

Seth Hopkins

Seth70810@aol.com

Brian Jenner

U.K.-based business speechwriter
info@tarsuscomms.co.uk

Marie Lerch

lerch_marie@bah.com

Mike Morrison

highlandercommunications@yahoo.com

Alan M. Perlman

Based in Highland Park, Illinois, Alan Perlman, a Ph.D. in linguistics, has 22 years' experience as a professional executive speechwriter.
alan@alanperlman.com
www.alanperlman.com

Dana Rubin

Provides a range of corporate communications and speechwriting services with a personal touch.
info@danarubin.com
http://www.danarubin.com

Jerry Tarver

jtarver@richmond.edu

Andrew Wilson

St. Louis–based corporate speechwriter
ABWilson@swbell.net

About the Author

John Kador is the author of seven business books, including *Charles Schwab: How One Company Beat Wall Street and Reinvented the Brokerage Industry* and *201 Best Questions to Ask on Your Interview*. *Net Ready: Strategies for Success in the E-conomy* (with Amir Hartman and John Sifonis) was a *New York Times* business bestseller. He is a corporate writer and has contributed over 1,000 articles to more than 50 business and technical publications. He received an M.S. degree in public relations from The American University and a B.A. in English from Duke University. He lives in Geneva, Illinois, with his wife and two children. He invites readers to contact him at jkador@jkador.com or visit his website www.jkador.com, where more resources for speechwriters may be found.